The Medes, the Persians and the Romans

Children's Middle Eastern History Books

Speedy Publishing LLC
40 E. Main St. #1156
Newark, DE 19711
www.speedypublishing.com

The Medes and Persians were originally from the central part of Asia. These Indo-European people moved to the western part of Asia around 1200 BC.

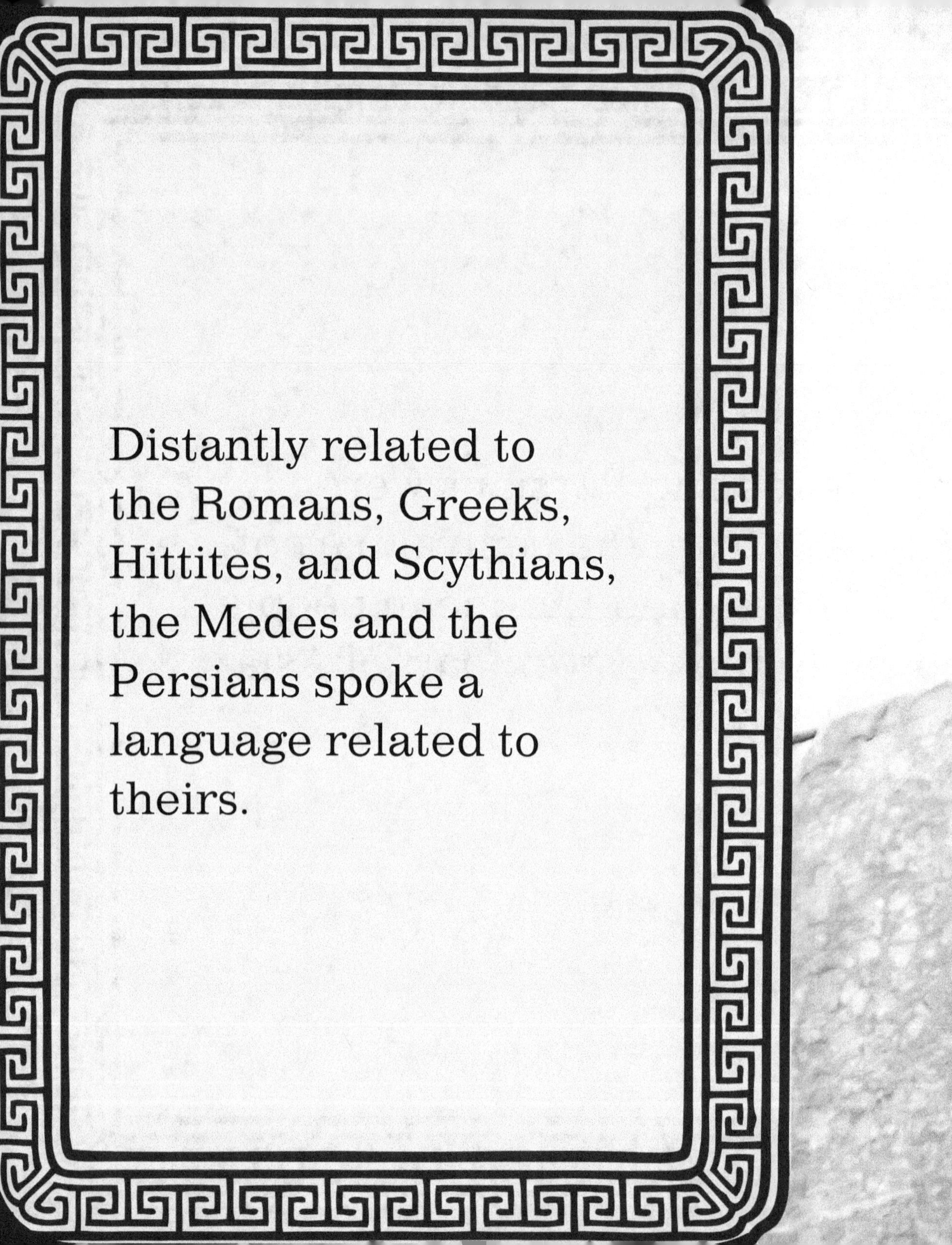

Distantly related to the Romans, Greeks, Hittites, and Scythians, the Medes and the Persians spoke a language related to theirs.

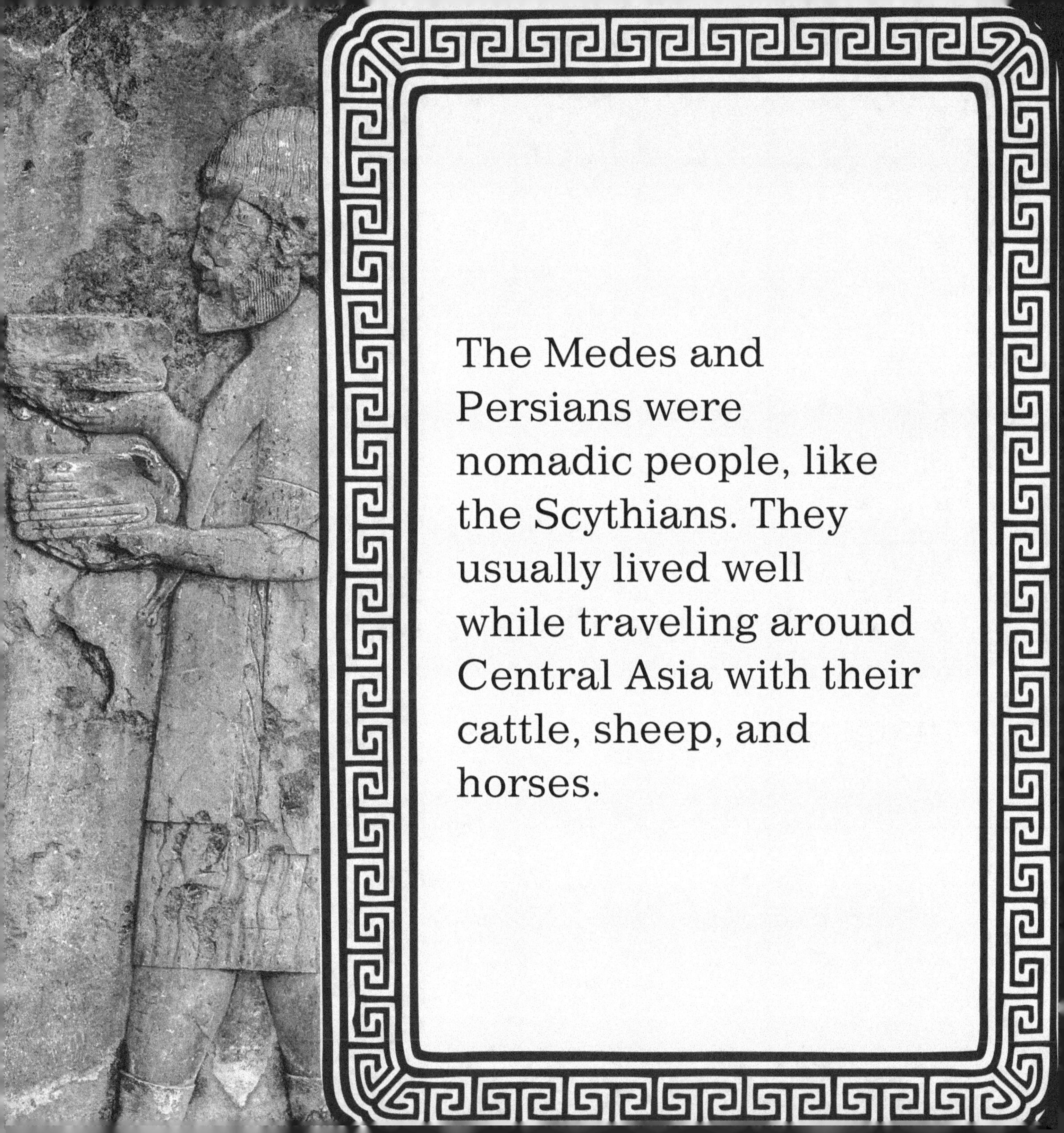

The Medes and Persians were nomadic people, like the Scythians. They usually lived well while traveling around Central Asia with their cattle, sheep, and horses.

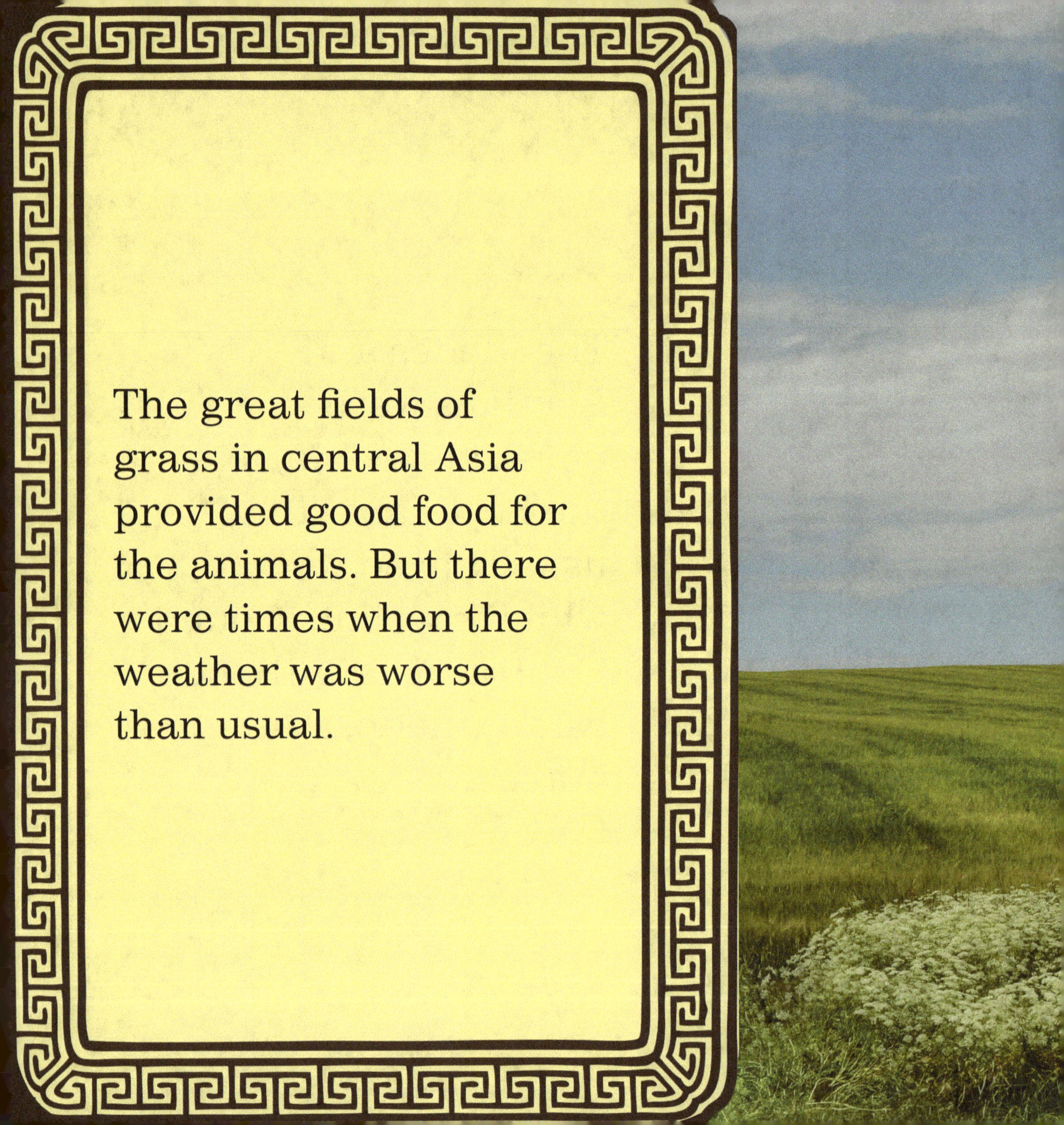

The great fields of grass in central Asia provided good food for the animals. But there were times when the weather was worse than usual.

This made it hard for the Medes and Persians to find enough food to eat. Because of this, the Medes and Persians traveled south into the western part of Asia. They settled in what is now known as Iran.

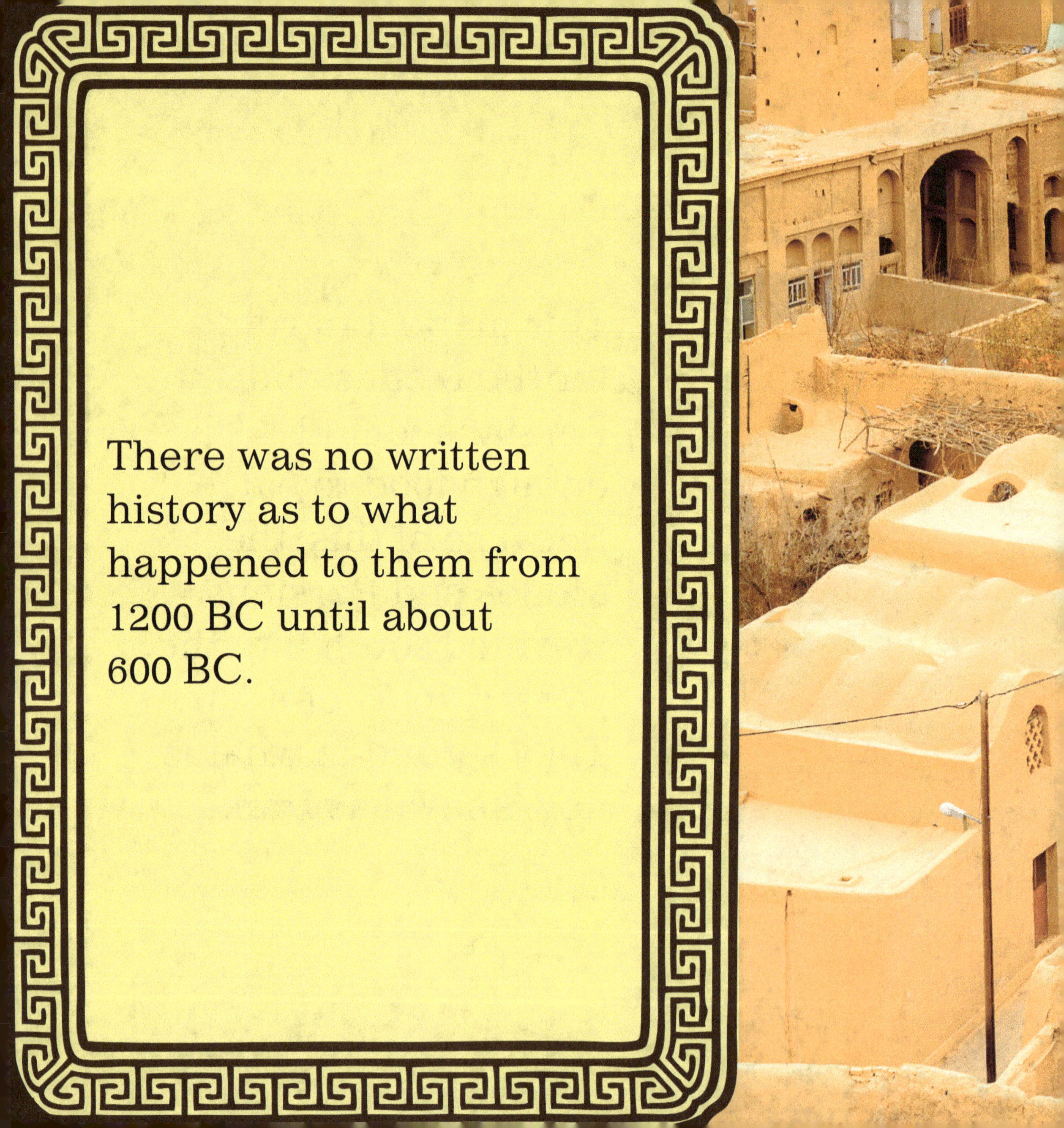

There was no written history as to what happened to them from 1200 BC until about 600 BC.

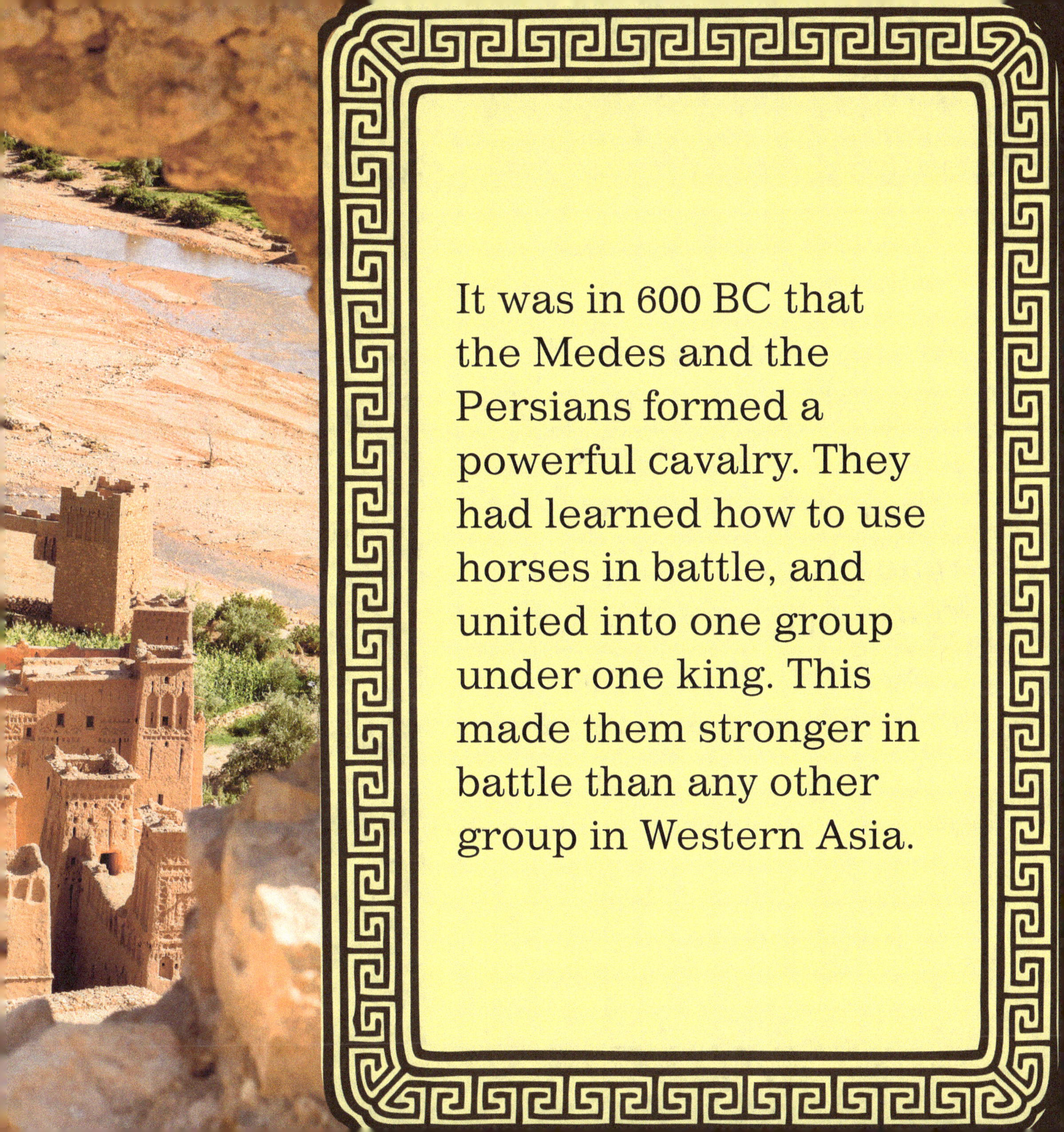

It was in 600 BC that the Medes and the Persians formed a powerful cavalry. They had learned how to use horses in battle, and united into one group under one king. This made them stronger in battle than any other group in Western Asia.

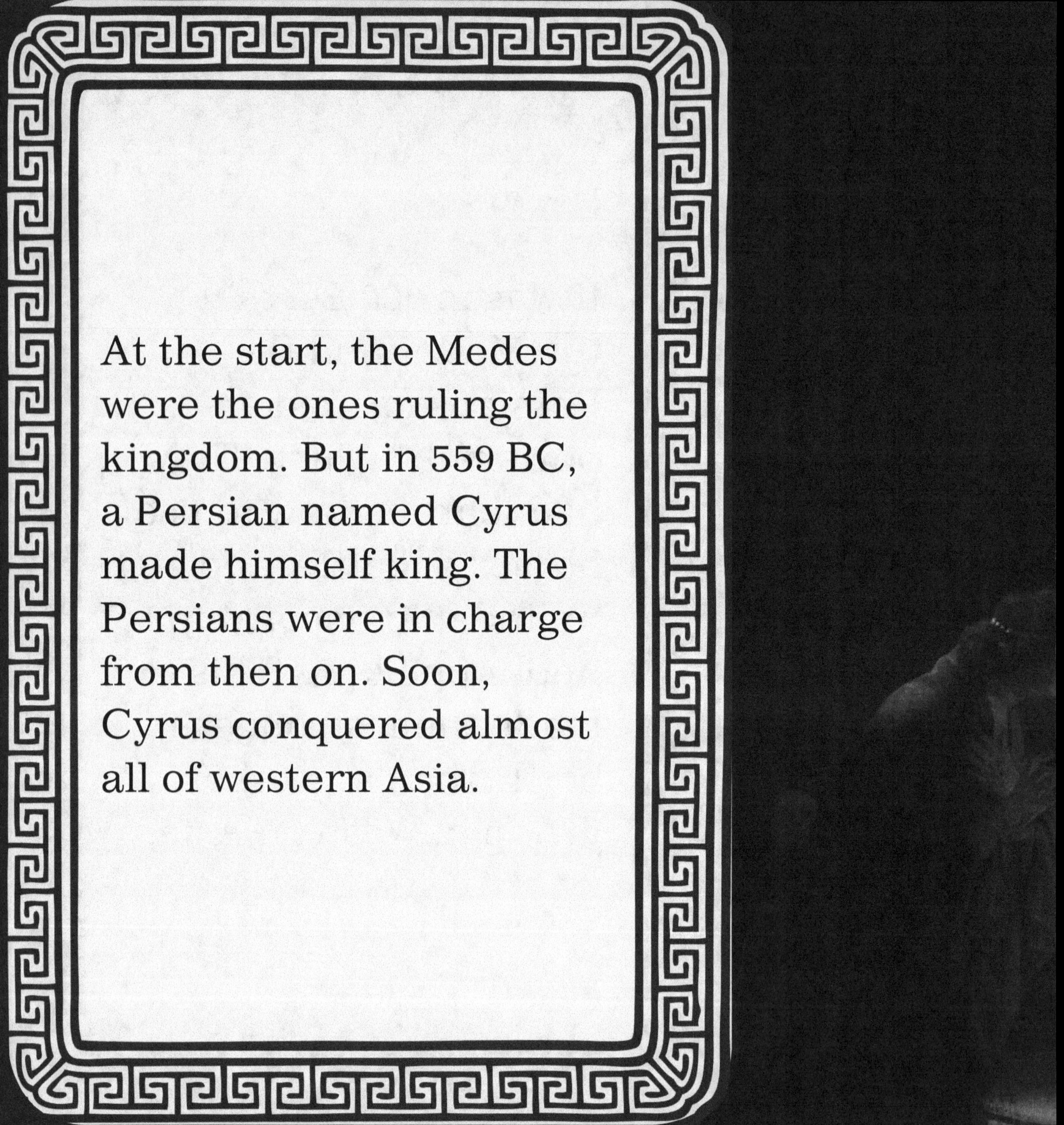

At the start, the Medes were the ones ruling the kingdom. But in 559 BC, a Persian named Cyrus made himself king. The Persians were in charge from then on. Soon, Cyrus conquered almost all of western Asia.

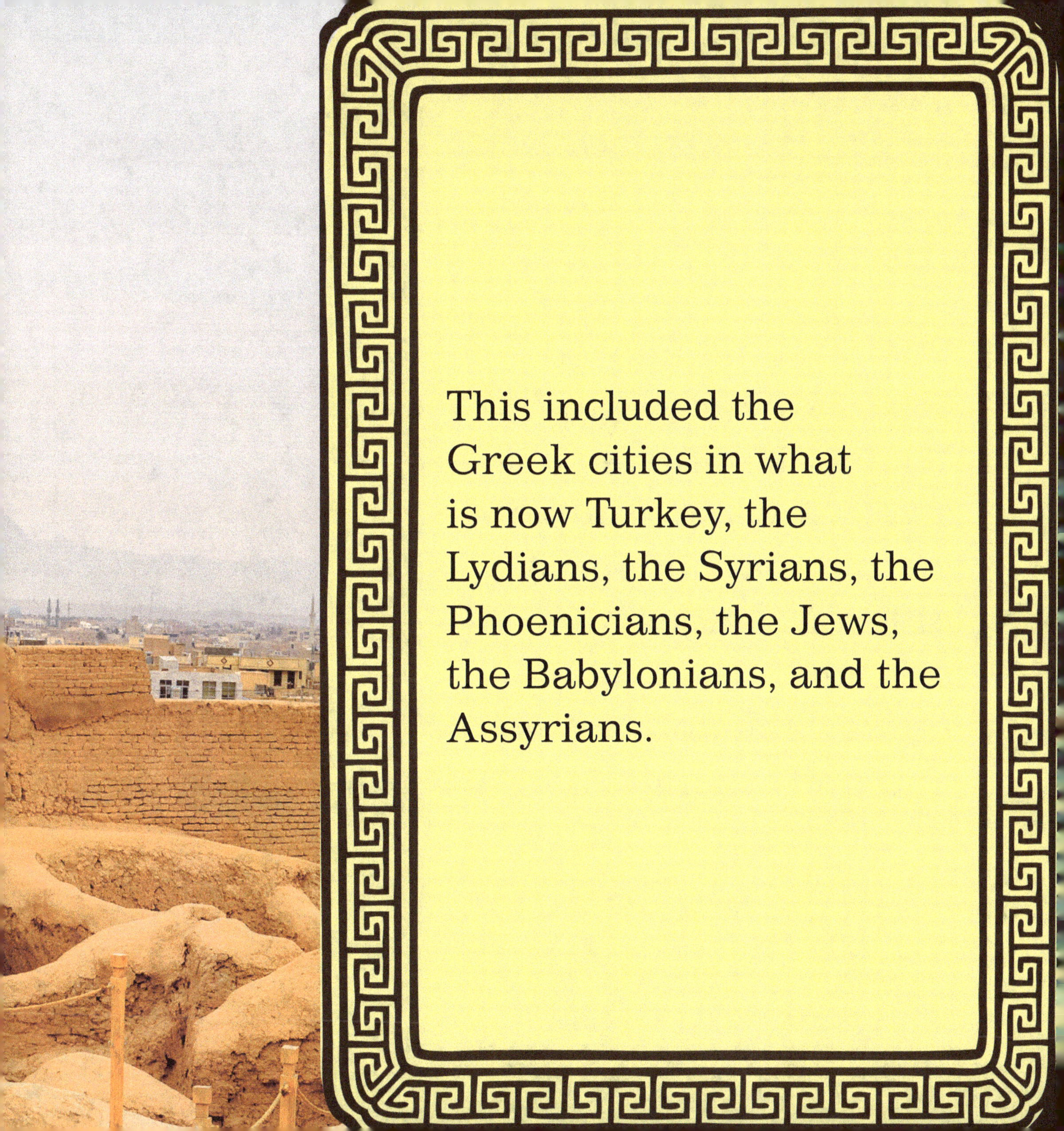

This included the Greek cities in what is now Turkey, the Lydians, the Syrians, the Phoenicians, the Jews, the Babylonians, and the Assyrians.

People remembered Cyrus as a good king. Though he reigned over a very diverse group of people that had many different languages, customs, and religions, he was able to manage and unify them.

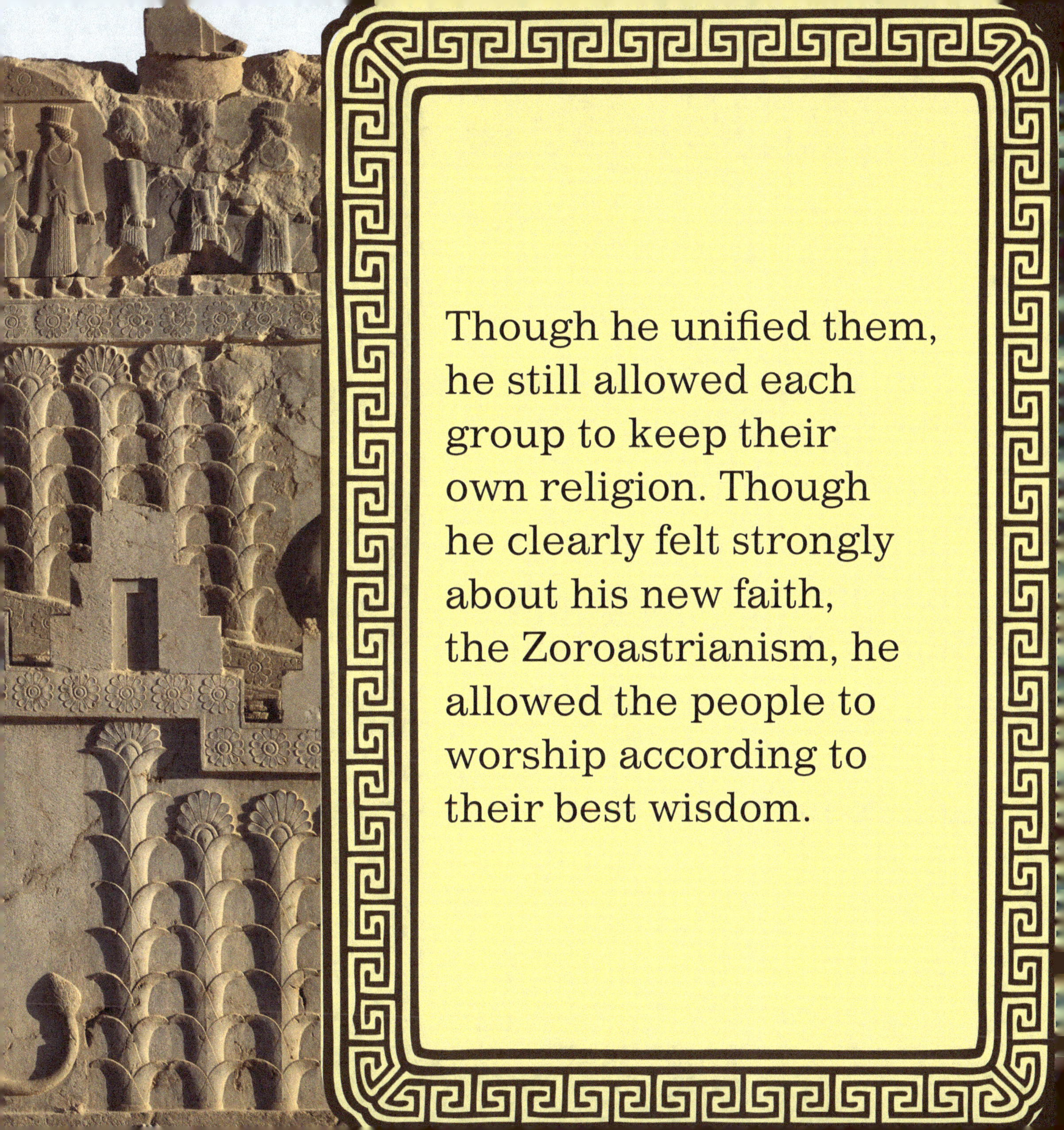

Though he unified them, he still allowed each group to keep their own religion. Though he clearly felt strongly about his new faith, the Zoroastrianism, he allowed the people to worship according to their best wisdom.

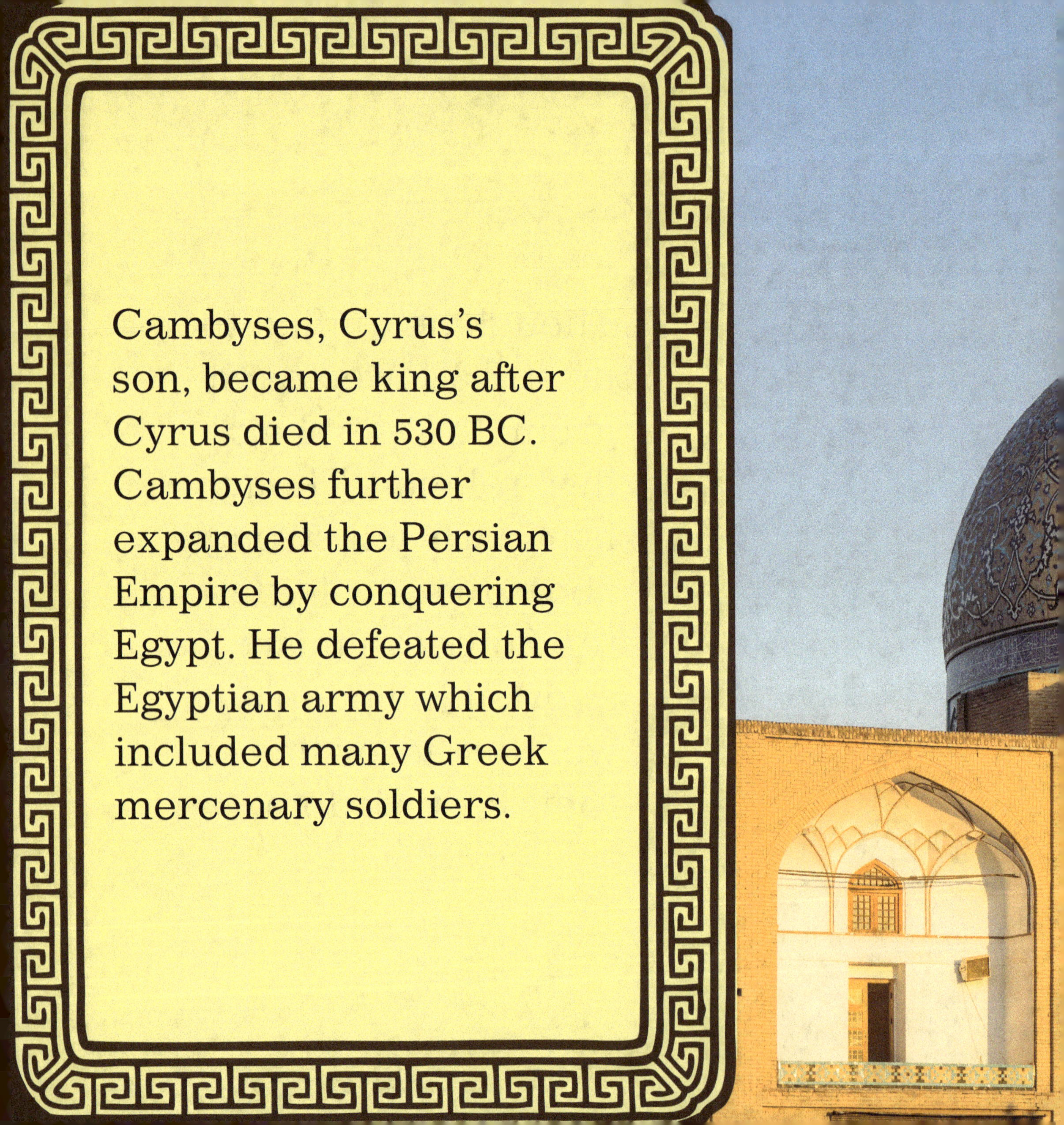

Cambyses, Cyrus's son, became king after Cyrus died in 530 BC. Cambyses further expanded the Persian Empire by conquering Egypt. He defeated the Egyptian army which included many Greek mercenary soldiers.

Later in life, Cambyses suffered from severe mental illness, and his own people eventually killed him, according to the historian Herodotus.

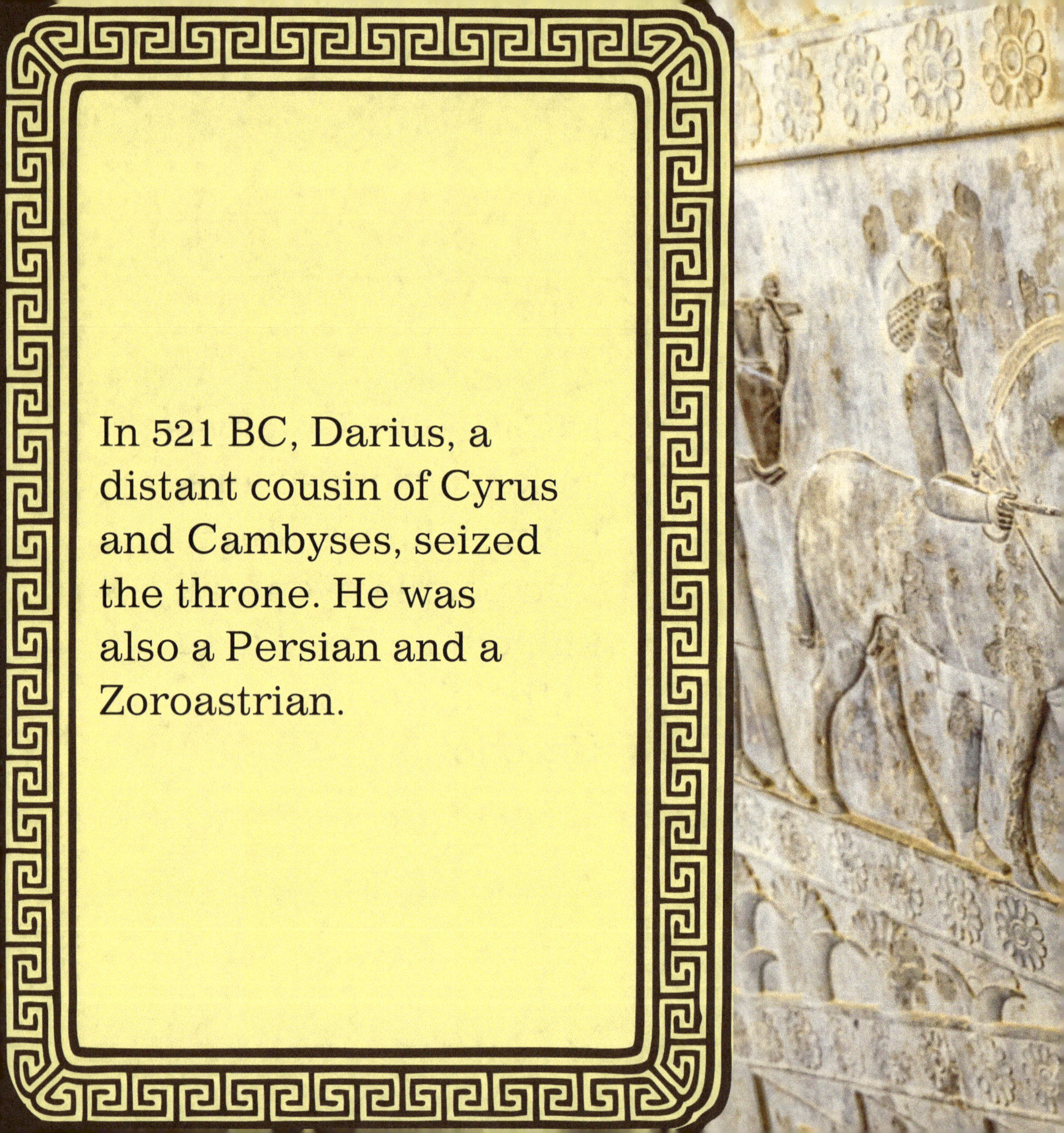

In 521 BC, Darius, a distant cousin of Cyrus and Cambyses, seized the throne. He was also a Persian and a Zoroastrian.

prominent family existed; it was rather like a clan. Firestone points out that "The development of the modern family meant the breakdown of a large, integrated society into small, self-centered units. The child within these conjugal units now became important" (Firestone 86). Albeit, with this importance, oppression of children is becoming more assertive, she writes. They are deprived of almost all legal rights. Women and children, thus, are oppressed together. The wife is oppressed by her husband; the child is oppressed by the father as such. *"Husband" and "father" are social roles which indicate oppression and male dominance*, she claims. Therefore, in a future world after the feminist revolution, children will have full legal rights (Firestone 234).

This idea reflects, on the one hand, the childhood of Firestone which was not quite pleasant. On the other hand, it exemplifies the idea of a "rebellion" against the male dominance (since children are treated neither as male nor as female, as she indicates). Obviously, such legal rights cannot be granted to children for many reasons. This is not a utopia but stupidity. Probably Firestone thinks of a kind of anarchy here- a society without rules and regulations. However, even if she has good intentions in her plans for a revolution, the idea of giving children the right to get married is dangerous and scandalous. As we said in the previous subchapter, this will open the door to legalization of the sexual abuse of children. Children are not mentally developed enough to be treated as adults. Perhaps the age of 21 can be lowered, but children under the age of 16 must be protected from adults' exploitation.

Now, by "protecting" the legal rights of children, Firestone believes that she will transform our society. The second demand of radical feminism, as she writes, is "full self-determination, including economic independence, of both women and children"

(Firestone 207). This can also be achieved employing "cybernetic socialism." As she adds, children can become independent not by working but by not working- labor will be unnecessary (Firestone 208).

Now, the picture is clear: women do not need marriage and children; and if they have children, they should be autonomous and not dependent upon men (in the role of a father, brother, son, husband, etc.). All current institutions need to be demolished- the Church, the state, the family, and the school. The primary purpose of school has been to maintain discipline, i.e., to oppress children. All their desires and ambitions are restricted and controlled. As Firestone claims, children are economically and physically oppressed; they are dependent. There is family repression, educational repression, sexual repression, and other types of it (she follows Freud here) (Firestone 96-99). Only children of the ghettos are free, although not absolutely.

Dworkin borrows these ideas from Firestone. The family imposes the incest taboo, which, according to Andrea Dworkin, is harmful to the individual. The family bonds need to be destroyed; incest will no longer exist because it can exist only in terms of family and the people outside of the family. As Dworkin puts it, "The destruction of the incest taboo is essential to the development of cooperative human community based on the free-flow of natural androgynous eroticism" (Dworkin 189). Her vision of the future is borrowed from Firestone: the two sexes should disappear and be replaced by an androgynous human being. Dworkin goes on with the offensive words that "The incest taboo can be destroyed only by destroying the nuclear family as the primary institution of the culture. The nuclear family is the school of values in a sexist, sexually repressed society" (Dworkin 190).

Dworkin here indicates another dimension of the problem of the family from the stance of radical feminism- the existence of two precisely defined sexes. She is eager to prove that "man" and "woman" are categories created by human beings. In this, she distinguishes herself from Firestone who did not go that far. Dworkin postulates the following: "'Man' and 'woman' are fictions, caricatures, cultural constructs. As models they are reductive, totalitarian, inappropriate to human becoming. As roles they are static, demeaning to the female, dead-ended for male and female both" (Dworkin 174). Culture is what legalizes them, what makes them legal and "normal", she writes. With this, she stands very close to the current development in feminism which recognizes the existence of many different genders and even of people who do not have any gender. Obviously, her solution to the problem of the inequality between men and women is simply to reject the existence of men and women as such!

Then Dworkin formulates her absurd thought as follows: "*We are, clearly, a multisexed species which has its sexuality spread along a vast fluid continuum where the elements called male and female are not discrete" (Dworkin 183).* In brief, there are no men and women, but persons who tend to be "more male" or "more female." In such a manner, the current status quo can be destroyed, and full equality will be achieved. As she declares, "We want to destroy sexism, that is, polar role definitions of male and female, man and woman." She then goes on by adding other institutions and concepts which, in her opinion, are harmful to women: "We want to destroy patriarchal power at its source, the family; in its most hideous form, the nation-state. We want to destroy the structure of culture as we know it, its art, its churches, its laws" (Dworkin 153). Even the current legislative system (and probably judicial system) are to be transformed or demolished. They serve the interests of men, of male dominance.

Nevertheless, they are not the only focus of Dworkin's onslaught on the "patriarchal system." She is very critical regarding sexual intercourse. This radical feminist states that "It means acting out the female role, incorporating the masochism, self-hatred, and passivity which are central to it. Unambiguous conventional heterosexual behavior is the worst betrayal of our common humanity" (Dworkin 184). With this, she also rejects all natural intercourse, thereby putting stress on homosexuality. The latter is a blow against male dominance because the latter is based on the intercourse between men and women. Once this "bipolarity" is eradicated, women will be able to decide whether to have intercourse with men or not.

Heterosexuality is to be avoided, as Dworkin states: "Homosexuality, because it is by definition antagonistic to two-sex polarity, is closer at its inception to androgynous sexuality" (Dworkin 185). Nonetheless, she admits that even homosexuality is based on the assumption of roles and that masculinity and femininity are present even in homosexual couples.

Following Firestone's conception of children as oppressed by their fathers, Andrea Dworkin claims that children stand close to the ideal of a human being without gender. She points out that "The distinctions between 'children' and 'adults,' and the social institutions which enforce those distinctions, would disappear as androgynous community develops" (Dworkin 192). In conclusion, she asserts without hesitation: "We must refuse to submit to those institutions which are by definition sexist —marriage, the nuclear family, religions built on the myth of feminine evil" (Dworkin 193). This opposition should lead to the eradication of the main differences between men and women, between masculine and feminine.

Why all this animosity toward the family? Radical feminists believe that men have established all institutions, including marriage and the family, in order to keep their power over women. Since women are biologically "handicapped" (due to the fact that they give birth to children and raise them), their only salvation is not to get married and not to enter romantic relationships with men. Only in such a manner can women be sure that they will not become pregnant and maintain their independence.

Like the case with pregnancy and children, here we can say that radical feminism enjoins doubt to a natural phenomenon. In some sense, the family has always existed- even if in the past, it was larger and covered many more connections and relations than today. In the Middle Ages, men dominated these extended families, which means that this is natural. The explanation is simple, and Andrea Dworkin is aware that men protected their households and settlements in ancient times. This is due to their physical strength and some psychological traits which make men better warriors than women. Not that women are unable to be warriors; some women in history were awe-inspiring (Saint Joan d'Arc). Women, however, are generally not equal to men when fighting without weapons. This is the historical reason why men have dominated our society and all societies before: to protect their families and relatives.

In the following chapter, we will analyze some contradictions and absurdities of radical feminism. Here we can say that radical feminists constantly contradict themselves. How can any type of feminism claim that sexes do not exist, and that they are a "construct"? The current state of scientific knowledge is that there are more than six thousand five hundred objective differences between men and women. If they are not real, why do feminists fight for more women's rights? If women are not really women, then who they are? What do they want?

Dworkin can say that feminism before her did not realize that the idea of sexes is wrong and that there are many sexes which cannot be defined succinctly. Nevertheless, if nature is not important here, and every person can feel as he/she wants, then every woman can become a man. Therefore, women can also participate in this "male dominance"!

Another idea of both Firestone and Dworkin sounds strange. Children do not have any gender, as they say. However, how can we define boys, then? Are boys something different than male human beings? They are male and not male at once, according to this interpretation. More recent feminists claim that boys are also part of the "scheme" of "male dominance." From childhood, they learn how to treat women and how to make them submit to their will. Therefore, boys are also male, and they cannot be entirely seen as innocent children, at least from the standpoint of Firestone and Dworkin.

There is no need to say that children can never be granted the same right as adults, for many reasons- biological, psychological, social, and so forth. Children themselves do not need such rights. They only need to have a normal childhood, to be allowed to play freely and to live peacefully, far away from war and poverty. Children are children for biological reasons; their bodies, brains, and psyches are still far from developed. This cannot be changed. We cannot transform the child into an adult. Moreover, if we treat children as adults, then the conception of maturity will lose its sense.

Julie Bindel is another representative of radical feminism. She has been working on topics such as the family, marriage, and homosexual relations since the 1980s. She is famous for her defense of lesbianism and the idea that women can be independent only by adhering to it. Her onslaught on marriage is rooted in her opinion that marriage only oppresses women. In this, she does not differ much from Firestone and Dworkin. In one of her articles for the British Leftist newspaper *The Guardian*, she argues against marriage by saying: "The institution of marriage is outmoded, patriarchal, and built on inequality" (Bindel, Marriage par. 2). To the objection that same-sex marriage was legalized in Britain, she replies that this does not make any difference since now marriage is out-of-date: "Same-sex couples were only invited to the marriage malarkey because it was a failing institution" (Bindel, Marriage par. 5).

Bindel does not adhere to the facts here. If marriage is not vital anymore, then why do same-sex couples have the ambition to legalize it in every part of the world? If it is not crucial in Britain, why was this legalization declared a significant success for the LGBT community? She simply cannot repudiate the objection; therefore, she changes her stance toward marriage. Nonetheless, why does she feel so much hatred toward marriage? Probably there are personal reasons. Marriage, she states, "Reinforces the notion of women as property" (Bindel, Marriage par. 8). As evidence, she refers to ancient practices which do not exist in Britain: "Forced marriage, child brides and polygamy all show how human rights violations of women and girls all too often come hand in hand with marriage" (Bindel, Marriage par. 9).

However, where is polygamy or child "marriages" in the United States? The law forbids them. Her argument actually shows that modern civilization has achieved a lot: it has protected the rights of women and children. The terrible phenomena mentioned by Bindel were real in the past; they are still real in many parts of the world. Nevertheless, the fact that marriage today excludes any physical violence means that institutions can change. There was slavery in the past, but now there is no widespread slavery, even in a metaphorical sense.

Contrary to what we see, Bindel still adheres to her adverse view of marriage: "Marriage involves three rings: engagement ring, wedding ring, suffering. The end of marriage is the only way to ensure true equality for all" (Bindel, Marriage par. 11). With this, she declares her ambition to end marriage as an institution. For her, marriage needs to be abolished; people should live only in a "partnership."

Perhaps Bindel is right if we refer to the distant past. Many women were forced to get married very young because they had to bear children early. Life expectancy was relatively short, and it was recommended to have children early (even at the age of 15-16). More children also meant more "home assistants", people who can work in the household or the workshop. Love was rarely the reason to get married. It is not by accident that so many great novels describe the story of a man and a woman who cannot get married because their parents did not allow it. Nonetheless, today most people are free to choose what to do with their life. No one forces anyone to get married. Parents are generally passive when it comes to marriage.

If there is something wrong with marriage today, this is only the fact that sometimes it is centered around emotions, around passion, not around true love. Especially young people are unable to realize the difference between love and passion, and they think that they should get married as quickly as possible. The family, marriage, and love build a triangle in which all sides are essential and cannot be removed. If one of them is missing, then the other will remain unstable.

All these remarks that have been discussed now lead only to one conclusion: the need for a feminist revolution. According to Firestone, Dworkin, and Bindel, this is the only solution to the inequality which they see in this world. What is this revolution?

2.3 The feminist revolution

Summary:

The idea of a future revolution is one of the pillars of radical feminism. Here we will turn again to Firestone and Dworkin's views of the transformation and revolution in favor of feminism. We will offer arguments that demonstrate this conception's inadequacy and the fact that it is full of contradictions. Finally, we will quote some arguments elaborated by the former radical feminist Jessica Cameron against this current of feminism.

Since Karl Marx' socialism influenced her, Shulamith Firestone predicted a feminist revolution. As she says, the socialist revolution failed because it was based on the stereotypes and models of male dominance. The failure of the Communist Revolution was caused by its "male-biased revolutionary analysis" (Firestone 212). On the other hand, the dystopian world of *1984* is a male world where all women have to become men (Firestone 213). These two options are not suitable for feminism. Women should not become men; women are not men. But communist leaders are all men; and even if there are women among them, they behave like men.

Karl Marx says that there is a permanent struggle between workers and capitalists. In the past, he states, no one realized this because the ideology of the dominating class made workers' minds blind. Ideology, thus, is fundamental in this struggle. Similarly to Marx, Firestone points out that the fight of feminism is also a fight for the correct *description* of the world. She quotes the French feminist Simone de Beauvoir as follows: "Representation of the world… is the work of men; they describe it from their own point of view, which they confuse with absolute truth" (de Beauvoir, quoted by Firestone 156). In short, all we know about the world represents men's view. Therefore, there is a "male view" and a "female view" of the world! The first task of feminism is to engage all women with the mission to end this ideology and to replace it with their own- the ideology of radical feminism.

Marx's conception of exploitation of the workers' class by the capitalists has been replaced with the assumption that women are exploited by men. It is called instead a subordination and even "slavery." Andrea Dworkin speaks of a "gynocide," which comes from the Greek word for woman. This term covers all types of violence regarding women, in all possible spheres. Dworkin gives as an example the Chinese tradition of foot binding- a terrible practice which did much harm to Chinese women in the past. She thus says that "Men, after all, nave throughout history resorted to gynocide as a stratagem of social control, as a tactical way of attaining/maintaining power." She goes on by asserting "That is the simple, compelling reality. There are only two other options:

women must seize power, or we must accomplish the transformation into androgyny" (Dworkin 191).

The main task of feminism is thus either revolution of "dictatorship of women." [7] Perhaps a radical feminist revolution is what feminism seeks. At any rate, male dominance should be put to an end: "The commitment to ending male dominance as the fundamental psychological, political, and cultural reality of earth-lived life is the fundamental revolutionary commitment" (Dworkin 17). This revolution is also seen as a transformation: "It is a commitment to transformation of the self and transformation of the social reality on every level" (Dworkin 17).

What she has in mind here are the following points, which we can distinguish in her work:

1. A change in the attitude and mentality of women- they must fight for their rights and against male dominance.

2. On a political level, women must organize themselves to react against any type of harm done to them because they are women.

3. On a cultural level, women must be engaged with ideology and try to disseminate "feminist values."

4. On a social level, they should demolish all "conservative" institutions such as religion, marriage, and the family,

---

[7] Dworkin does not employ such a phrase, but her thought is quite similar to Marx's idea of a dictatorship of the *proletariat*.

5. Removing the strict definitions of women and men, of gender, of the fact that there are only two sexes, and moving in the direction of androgyny, or a human being which is male and female at once.

Indeed, the reader can become confused about all this. Is feminism a revolutionary ideology, or does it seek only a transformation of society? The language of Dworkin is quite Marxist. As we noted, feminism simply replaces the workers' class with the class of women (or sex class), showing that this is the primary division of humankind- men and women fight with each other. Race, ethnicity, religion, social background do not matter here, according to Dworkin: "Women are oppressed as women, regardless of class or race; some women have access to significant wealth, but that wealth does not signify power; women are to be found everywhere, but own or control no appreciable territory" (Dworkin 23). Women's revolution is the only way out of this situation, according to her.

Speaking about culture and ideology, both Firestone and Dworkin believe that male dominance is expressed through an ideology created by men and for men. We already mentioned this point earlier. This ideology is found not only in movies and books but also in fairytales. The most popular fairytales need to be removed and forgotten because women are shown negatively. Andrea Dworkin states the following: "Cinderella, Sleeping Beauty, Snow-white, Rapunzel- all are characterized by passivity, beauty, innocence, and *victimization*…They never think, act, initiate, confront, resist, challenge, feel, care, or question. Sometimes they are forced to do housework" (Dworkin 42). All they are good women, as she notes. Therefore, a revolution must be violent; all women will become "bad," in the sense that they will stand against the rules formulated by men. This revolution will have social, economic, political, cultural aspects.

The idea of a feminist revolution has been defined better by Firestone. Her vision of a future society without significant differences between men and women is explicitly formulated in her works. Now, we should subject this conception to criticism. Here are the following arguments against a possible feminist revolution:

1. A revolution is never the solution. Historically, revolutions have turned out to be harmful or even devastating. Two examples of this fact are the French Revolution (1789) and the Russian (Communist) Revolution in 1917.

2. It is impossible to oppose women to men on the ground of gender. We are all connected and related to people from the other gender. Men do not live alone, only with men; at least, men have mothers, so they are in contact with women.

3. Marx's conception of a communist revolution indicated that there would not be capitalism and capitalists in the future. They should be eradicated. Feminism could not insist on such a view about men, because a world without men is impossible to think. Men are needed, at least for the reproduction of humankind.

4. Radical feminists always mix nature with nurture. They say that the division of men and women is natural and cultural at the same time. So, which factor is more decisive: nature or culture? If nature is more potent, then a revolution will not achieve its goal. If culture is more substantial, then there is no need for a revolution- it is enough to change the mentality of human beings to make them treat women better.

5. Androgynous human beings will never appear on earth. We are men and women; a state in-between these two genders is not a real state, it is a result of a psychical disorder. We cannot become men and women concurrently, in one body. Probably this can be achieved through technologies, but even then it will not be very certain that these beings are really human. The manufactured entity would not be authentic or ontologically accurate. Firestone says that the revolution will create an androgynous culture; it will reintegrate Male with Female (Firestone 190). Nevertheless, this is an entirely different thing: she speaks more of culture than of nature. Male and female are not the same as men and women. There is something female in every man, and in every woman, there is something male- this cannot be doubted. Nevertheless, men remain men, and women remain women.

6. A feminist revolution aiming at creating an androgynous society will mean that women and the female will be eradicated as such. There will not be women anymore. So what is the sense of such a revolution? Instead of being granted more rights and liberties, women will simply cease to exist.

7. If this will be a violent revolution, how can it be conducted in practice? How can women defeat men with weapons? Will this mean that women become soldiers and organize themselves into armies? Will women devote themselves entirely to becoming inventors and military engineers?

8. What about children? As we noted, boys are also male, so the revolution will target them as well. What will the "revolutionaries" do with boys? Will they be persecuted?

No doubt, all these arguments cannot be repudiated by radical feminists. The only thing which they offer us are emotions, and the strongest of them is hatred. There is nothing of the sort of love, tenderness, solidarity, empathy, compassion. Even Marx speaks of solidarity between workers. Furthermore, his ideas of class struggle are a little bit closer to the truth, since people are really distributed in social classes. Poor people live together with poor people, wealthy people with wealthy ones. However, men and women do not live separately. This is perhaps the biggest factual mistake of radical feminism. Firestone is unable to realize this fact: *men and women are together and should be together. There is nothing of the kind of class struggle here*. Marx speaks of workers taking the whole production and financial benefit for themselves; but how can women engage in all human activities without the help of men?

Firestone's vision of the future world is absolutely unclear. Marx at least tries to depict the state of the communist society in the future. He shows a classless society, in which workers dominate and have all means of production in their hands. They have absolute power- political, economic, and social. Following him, radical feminism should depict a society without men. Nevertheless, Firestone and her fellows understand quite well that this is impossible. Furthermore, this is what makes their feminist revolution a utopia.

There is another, an ethical point that needs to be considered carefully by everyone who follows the ideals of radical feminism. The feminist revolution is also a moral transformation. As a matter of fact, our morality will be eradicated. We do not know what will be the new "revolutionary" values. One should be afraid even to think of them after reading Firestone's shocking words that the incest taboo and the ban on child marriage should be removed. Writing about the future society, Firestone points out that there will be a transitional period during which some practices of living in a family will remain and will be maintained. However, eventually, humankind will reach the stage when "our psychosexual structures may become altered so radically that the monogamous couples… would become obsolescent." Monogamy can be replaced by "transexual group marriages which also involved older children" (Firestone 229). She, however, expresses her uncertainty here, so this remains only her hypothesis. But the very fact that she assumes something of the type of marriage with children is terrible; it only shows that radical feminism is not feminism at all because it destroys women, womanhood, and consequently, children!

It should be noted, however, that radical feminism is not that radical in all of its points. For instance, Andrea Dworkin has fought against pornography and prostitution. Her conviction, and also of her fellows, is that these phenomena are related to male dominance. In short, men established these "institutions" in order to hurt women and to make them more vulnerable. This, of course, is not true, because pornography has existed since the beginning of the 20th century, and this does not have anything to do with traditional morality. It is merely the result of the lack of morality, or a moral vacuum, as it can be called.

About prostitution, it can be said that in the past, it had some weighty connection to the higher classes. At any rate, prostitution is banned in many countries belonging to the so-called Western civilization. This is a decision taken mainly by men; so no one can prove that alleged "male dominance" is the reason for the existence of this negative phenomenon. All this, to repeat, ensues from a lack of morality and from the radical transformation of our society. *Today people prefer to have pleasures and wealth over strong family ties, love, and a stable family. This is one of the characteristics of our globalized world dominated by the consumer culture and the idea that everything can be bought.*

Plenty of absurdities in radical feminism will be analyzed further. Here we can say that some representatives of this movement have distanced themselves from it because of all these contradictions and shocking views. Jessica Jay Cameron, already mentioned here, is one of them. However, she was influenced by socialism, which made her feel skeptical about radical feminism. As she says, "Socialist feminism taught me that gender is not the only axis of oppression" (Cameron 4). Another source of her work is the so-called sex-positive feminism. This is a current which holds onto the idea that heterosexual relationships are appropriate, and that there is no need for women to treat all men as oppressors. As she writes, "Sex-positive feminism enabled me to investigate gendered sexual practices without an obsessive focus on injury" (Cameron 4).

To be sure, there is no precise definition of this current. It can be said that "sex-positive feminism" and "sex-negative feminism" belong to radical feminism; they both exist within its ideological framework. The difference is simply that one of them is less radical. Cameron and her fellows do not put intense stress on women's victimization and the idea that male dominance is absolute and penetrates every sphere of human activity. They also do not frequently employ the word "patriarchal." Influenced also by a philosophical movement typical of the second half of the last century- poststructuralism (mainly developed by French philosophers such as Levi-Strauss), she claims that "poststructural feminism provided relief from the political weight of structural analyses of patriarchy's "truth" (Cameron 4).

Jessica Cameron contrasts both types of radical feminism to each other, claiming that sex-positive feminism does not have anything to do with radical feminism. As she remarks, "Radical feminism…was vocal in pointing out the wrongs of sexuality as practised under patriarchal social relations" (Cameron 4). She adds that "heterosexual intercourse was too often an exercise in male hedonism, sexual assault was all-pervasive, and pornography and sex work, as reflections of unequal social relations, served male pleasure no matter the costs to women." This means the relations of women with men are seen as wrong and are forbidden. The other current, to which Cameron belongs, perceives these relations as potentially suitable for women, if they are not forced to enter them. She observes that "Sex-positive feminism, conversely, frequently focused on the wrongs of radical feminism. Here, the concern was erasures of female sexual pleasure through an overemphasis on sexual danger" (Cameron 4).

Radical feminism also emphasizes the patriarchal society and refuses to accept that this society does not exist anymore, that it has passed away. Jessica Cameron observes the following: "Understanding all heterosexual encounters as heavily contextualized, or even determined, by patriarchal social relations overshadows possibilities for pleasure and play" (Cameron 16). Radical feminism rejects the possibility for the existence of normal romantic relationships.

Cameron sees another weak point in the works of Firestone and her fellows. She thinks that radical feminism is based entirely on ideology, and it puts a too strong emphasis on the idea of a revolution. According to the Marxist definition of ideology, "it is a false set of ideas used to conceal unjust material relations in the interests of the ruling class or, in this case, the ruling gender. Ideology is placed in opposition to knowledge, which is equated with freedom, progress, or liberation" (Cameron 7). Contrary to this, poststructuralism pays more heed to the narrative, to the storytelling. As Cameron puts it, it has an interest in the genealogy of concepts: "Here, the focus becomes the social *implications* of the stories we tell and the ideas we hold rather than fixed structures and truths. The lineage of concepts, institutions, and social practices becomes more important than discovering their cause" (Cameron 7). In short, there is no strict causality in the world of storytelling, in what we call culture and society. Only what a certain thing means and what the implications of the use of the particular word are is what is of any import.

As the reader is able to see now, there are different types of feminism. Furthermore, even in radical feminism, one can find different camps fighting with each other. Contemporary feminism is not homogenous; it is far from any agreement on any problem. Cameron thus admits that "it is difficult both to draw clear lines between different feminist frameworks and to attribute unified political positions to any particular feminism. Feminist frameworks and the political positions attributed to them are often contested" (Cameron 14). This should not prevent us from criticizing the particular works of Firestone, Dworkin, Bindel, and their fellows. All absurdities and weird ideas found in them need to be countered instead of being ignored.

2.4 Conclusion

Classical feminism is so different from radical feminism that one can even doubt whether the latter can be called feminism at all. Radical feminism offers a new approach to the problems addressed by feminism in general. It does not demand gender equality; it demands female dominance, and if possible, a new society in which men will be wholly subordinated to women. This is a society without families, marriage, monogamy, incest taboo; a society in which women will be allowed to do whatever they want in all senses, including a sexual sense. This is not even a matriarchy; it does not have anything familiar with this ancient order of society.

The feminist revolution is seen as something similar to the communist revolution. There cannot be a doubt that the influence of Marx over radical feminism is the strongest. Marxism aims at destroying the current social and political order, thereby replacing them with the power of the workers. Feminism employs the word “women” instead of “workers.” However, it is quite wrong in one aspect: a revolution of all women against all men is impossible.

The weak point of radical feminism is that it says there is some problem, something wrong, but it does not offer an accurate solution. It does not have any nexus point with reality. Marxism at least was based on some factual evidence and economical analysis (although many of its conclusions were wrong). Radical feminists simply have stated that classical feminism is nothing, it did not achieve anything, and women need another ideology to help them achieve “salvation” from “male dominance.” Its attitude toward the feminists before it is arrogant and cynical; it merely says that it is the inspiration of women nowadays, and no one and nothing else can do anything good for them.

Nevertheless, these are not the only weak points of contemporary feminism. There are more contradictions which can be seen in the works of its proponents. We will turn now to contemporary feminism as comprising all currents which have emerged in recent decades.

Chapter III: The contradictions of contemporary feminism

Contemporary feminism is complicated to define. There are so many currents within it that we could get lost if we tried to elaborate a precise definition of it. Furthermore, within these currents, there are also different views regarding the same issues. This turns feminism into a diverse movement. However, in the present work, we have attempted to point to several vital views which, according to us, are characteristic of all feminist currents. To be sure, there are exceptions- there can be some feminists that do not agree, for example, with the idea that the family should be abolished. Nevertheless, all feminists agree that our society is dominated by the so-called patriarchal values, practices, and mentality.

It is time now to move forward, to one very interesting aspect of feminism. This is its logical and practical contradictions, which are easy to see from without. There is one unwritten rule regarding social and political movements: the more radical it becomes, the more absurdities and contradictions it consists of. In the case of radical feminism, we can assert that *it leads us to very disputable and even shocking ideas*. We have seen by now some of these "solutions"- to abolish the family, to remove the differences between the genders, to give full rights to children, to transform our society into an androgynous society, and so forth.

On the other hand, the so-called liberal feminism does not go that far. It is more critical toward radical feminism, but they agree that society's transformation is needed. They both say that our society needs to be changed and that women should be empowered to remove male domination. For instance, Julie Bindel, whom we referred to earlier, does not belong to radical feminism herself; some of her ideas could be ascribed to this current (that homosexuality stands closer to human nature). However, in other aspects, she criticizes the revolutionary passion of Andrea Dworkin and her radical fellows. In this chapter, we will see that Bindel offers a sober interpretation of some absurdities and paradoxes found in contemporary feminism.

There are three central points to be discussed here: (1) rejection of gender equality, (2) approval of the anti-women practices of Islam, and (3) rejection of femininity. As it will be demonstrated here, radical feminism arrives at a stage in which it contradicts itself and repudiates its own postulates.

3.1 Against gender equality

Summary:

The first paradox of feminism is its insistence on the equal number of men and women in every profession. As we demonstrated, this would be disastrous to both men and women. Absolute equality in terms of numbers means that some skilled and gifted men or women should leave their job.

In its initial form, feminism fought for women's rights. It claimed that men and women should be granted equal rights because all human beings are born equal (the theory of natural rights). Over time, feminism began demanding more and more: better jobs for women, better positioning in society, more comprehensive access to education. Currently, some of its demands are to remove the pay-gap, to have equal numbers of women in all institutions of executive, judicial, and legislative power, and to force businesses to accept more women among the top-ranked managers. If we consider the weird ideas of Firestone and Dworkin, then we can add the feminist revolution and radical transformation of society by removing the gender differences.

Where is gender equality and gender balance in all we have read in authors such as Andrea Dworkin? All we can see is that men are responsible for everything terrible that befalls women; men are guilty even without committing any crime. Men's original sin is that they are born men, male, which means, aggressive and violent. As Dworkin herself explains, men have taken advantage of the fact that women become pregnant and must look after children, so men simply took power in their hands and began their domination over women. Women have had to submit to men's will without their own consent. By using physical violence and by legalizing this violence, men have been able to dominate and to have full control.

One of the examples of this given in the book of Dworkin is Chinese footbinding. According to her, this terrible practice was created by men for men. Men had to enjoy the beauty of women's feet, so they "invented" a unique conception of beauty to be maintained in Chinese society. Footbinding is called by Dworkin *gynocide*, because it has lead to the death and illness of millions of women in the past. It can lead to severe injuries not only of women's feet but also of other parts of the body. Nevertheless, instead of accusing this Chinese tradition, Dworkin directly attacks all men in the world for the existence of this practice.

In her opinion, men needed to dominate, so they had to create some differences between the genders. Women and men are not different by nature, so all differences which we see now are "cultural." As she suggests, "Footbinding was a visible brand.

Footbinding did not emphasize the differences between men and women —it created them, and they were then perpetuated in the name of morality" (Dworkin 103). She adds that "One sex became male by virtue of having made the other sex some thing, something other, something completely polar to itself, something called female" (Dworkin 107). In such a way, men drew a sharp line between men and women, masculine and feminine, domination and submission.

The history of humankind is a history of oppression and slavery of women, as Firestone and Dworkin believe. This is a history of an unequal struggle between two classes, men and women. Dworkin asks the following question: "Why everywhere the oppression of women throughout recorded history? How could the Inquisitors torture and bum women as witches? How could men idealize the bound feet of crippled women? How and why?" (Dworkin 110-11). Her explanation is simply that this is men's nature: to dominate and to behave sadistically. Many feminists like her agree with that: men are born with a disposition toward aggression and violence; men are much more aggressive than women because this is natural to them.

Ironically, feminists turn to biology when this is in their favor; otherwise, they would speak of "social construction" and "cultural factors." So here they claim the following: men are born with testosterone; this makes them aggressive, and this could not be controlled. Men start wars to "satisfy" their "aggressive instincts." Albeit, when there is no war, they are still violent, mainly regarding women as their wives, sisters, mothers, or daughters. Because they feel uncomfortable with this fact, men have established this practice as moral and say that women's subordination is natural. So men are aggressive in many aspects: physical, social, political, cultural (which also includes religion), etc.

No doubt, the history of humanity is full of wars and armed conflicts. In most cases, men are involved. Nevertheless, the reason for this is not genetic; it is far from biological. The truth is simply that in the past, there were many wars; perhaps human beings were not as civilized as they are now. But we cannot blame it on biology or nature. If men are biologically aggressive, how did the current civilization emerged? Why are men not that aggressive nowadays? This simply indicates that we cannot rely entirely on biology or culture when we try to explain human behavior. This is a well-proven fact, and these feminists repudiate it without reason.

Now, we arrive at another point. Women are allegedly oppressed, so they must fight for equality. How do feminists envisage this? For them, equality is merely numerical: the number of men in Congress should be equal to women. There is nothing wrong in the idea of equal access to Congress, but how can we enforce legally a given quota of women to enter Congress? This means many gifted men who have been prepared to work as congressmen should be rejected only because of this false equality! Women's chances to enter Congress will be much better, and this merely because of their gender, not due to their experience or education!

Such equality can be achieved in another way. More women should be admitted to political parties. Then it is the will of the voters who will decide who will become a member of Congress. However, this should not be carried out forcefully, by throwing many talented men out of the election campaigns.

To understand the absurdity of all this, we can turn to a fictive example. It is well known that most teachers in the United States (and generally in the world) are women. If we introduce the concept of gender equality in education, then half of the teachers should be men. With this, many talented female teachers would be deprived of the opportunity to work. They will be either forced to go to another town or state, or simply resign and find another job. Furthermore, how can we define the criteria who should become a teacher and who not? Who can guarantee that the male teachers "added" to a given school because of this new bill will be able to teach properly?

Thus, the reader can realize that the idea of absolute gender equality in all professions is wrong. There should be open access to people from both genders, but not forceful equality. Currently, feminism is speaking of "gender balance." The difference is that balance here does not mean complete equality. The number of men should not be equal to women, but more women should be admitted to the so-called "male" professions, and more men- to "female" professions. More women should be encouraged to become engineers, soldiers, aircraft pilots; more men should become teachers, nurses, PRs, and so forth. Gender balance has replaced gender equality.

The latter is what rational feminists declare. Unfortunately, radical feminists do not agree. For them, women should have all the power- not merely be empowered. Women should be presidents of different states, women should be heads of international organizations, and women should care more about the lives of women around the world. Persons like Hilary Clinton should be president of the United States simply because she is a woman, not because of her skills and knowledge or her political views. It is good that American citizens realized how wrong this approach is and did not overwhelmingly vote for her (2016).

The broader participation of women in the political process is achievable through education. By training young women to become politicians and by admitting them into political parties, the way to achieve this will be open.

Where is the contradiction here? the reader might ask. Feminism fights for the equality of men and women; at the same time, it refuses to give any privileges to men. Women should dominate, because in the past they were subordinated. That is, men should be enslaved in the new society. This is the standpoint of radical feminists. Even if we do not take into account this weird idea, the conception of gender equality remains. Such equality is not to be achieved, except by force. Nevertheless, feminism is based on the idea of individual liberty. *Why should all men be deprived of the opportunity to have a given job only because they are men*?

The solution to all this is straightforward. Feminism should speak of equal and open access to specific jobs, instead of forcing employers to admit a fixed number of women to this job. People should be treated according to their education, knowledge, experience; gender should not be taken into account here. Even the idea of "positive discrimination" is wrong, because it can only lead to injustice and lack of fairness. In the United States, women have many opportunities in front of them; no one forbids them to enter a given profession or to choose their workplace. Our legislation prohibits discrimination based on gender; hence it is not possible for an employer to deny a job to a woman simply because of her gender. Women are granted all rights in this country, and no one wants to deprive them of these rights. Nothing more can be done in this direction: as we already explained, if the number of women is equal to men in all professions, then this will be disastrous not only for men but also for women (as in the example with the teachers).

This is the first paradox or contradiction of feminism. It has ensued from a wrong interpretation of the idea of equal rights. Equal rights do not mean that all human beings should become the same, that they should be identical (this is a reduction to absurdity and is not cogent); it does not mean that men should be discriminated. In such a way, feminism stands against the principle of equality. In the next subchapter, we will discuss another example related to this fact.

3.2 Feminism in support of Islam

Summary:

This subchapter deals with the paradox of feminists accepting the practices of sharia law, which violates women's rights. Gabby Aossey will be presented here as a feminist author defending the right to wear the hijab. Julie Bindel opposes her by showing that Islam, and particularly sharia law are entirely anti-women. She is among the few feminists who realize the danger of sharia law.

Before we analyse this paradox, it is important to pay attention to two facts:

1. Islam and Muslims are not the same things. Islam is a religion, which means, a set of beliefs, rituals, and practices based on a religious worldview and sacred books.

Muslims are people belonging to this religion. When we speak of feminism defending Islam, we do not refer simply to Muslims, but to all doctrines of Islam.

2. Islam should not be taken as bad in itself; however, there are elements in it which should make every feminist worried. Here we will discuss precisely to these elements, not to all beliefs of Islam. All this given the fact that Islam in itself is not a monolithic religion but is divided into various currents (the main disciplines/branches are Shia and Sunni Islam).

The attitude of contemporary feminism toward religion is negative. Religion, as we will see in the next chapter, is usually ridiculed. Feminists such as Shulamith Firestone, Andrea Dworkin, or Julie Bindel declare themselves atheists. They believe that Christianity is the driving force of the modern patriarchal system that is still at work in our society. Christianity, they are convinced, is the "guardian" of patriarchal morality and practices, which means it "guards" men's domination over women.

One expects from contemporary feminism, then, to also reject Islam, since, Islam today stands firmly behind plenty of practices in which we see how women are discriminated. In Saudi Arabia, until recently, women could not drive a car. This is a simple example of the dominating treatment of women in Muslim societies. In Saudi Arabia and Iran, women cannot do virtually anything without the consent of their husbands or parents (in some cases, brothers). They are forced to marry without knowing their husbands; they are forced to submit to these men; they must tolerate the fact that their husbands can have four wives (officially allowed by Islam). Violence against women is officially prohibited in Muslim countries, but the practice shows that physical violence occurs very often in some families, and women simply have to get used to it.

What is worse, women themselves believe that they did something wrong, and that is why they are beaten or poorly treated. To all this, we can add the fact that girls under the age of 14 can "get married" in some countries. A survey by the PEW Research Center shows that most countries in the world allow for child marriage under certain circumstances. 192 countries out of 198 have stipulated when it is allowed for citizens to get married. Six countries do not have a minimum age, among them being Saudi Arabia, South Sudan and Somalia (Gray par. 5).

Nevertheless, in Sudan, girls can marry at the age of 10 (Gray par. 11). In Tanzania, a predominantly Muslim country, "Muslim and Hindu girls can marry at 12 as long as the marriage is not consummated until the girl reaches the age of 15" (Gray par. 13). However, setting a minimum age does not guarantee that the law will be observed. As the survey shows, "In Afghanistan, the legal minimum age for marriage is 16 (or 15 with the consent of a parent or guardian and the court) for girls and 18 for boys. However, international and local observers continued to report widespread forced and early marriage" (Gray par. 15).

This is only one of the examples of bad practices found in Muslim countries (not in all Muslim countries, but predominantly in them). It is entirely reasonable to think that feminists will stand for the rights of these young girls and will protect them from forceful marriage. However, do they do it?

Contemporary feminists, whether liberal or radical ones, rarely address the problem of gender discrimination in Muslim countries and societies. This is a problem that concerns not only Muslim countries but also Western societies due to the massive number of Muslims residing in them. It cannot be said that this is a problem of Muslims themselves since they are part of our society. Western countries (meaning, the United States and Europe) have stipulated specific regulations regarding women's rights. In the United States and Europe, women's rights are completely protected and defended in many ways: through legislation, through the judicial system, and in the spheres of culture, science, morality, and religion. No one can stand against the law.

Unfortunately, feminists do not care too much about the lives of Muslim women. Alternatively, if they are solicitous for women, it is not shown in the proper way or adequately. Feminists today are affiliated with Leftism. It happens very often that they organize marches against racism and xenophobia. They take part in campaigns against Islamophobia as well. Some of the organizers are Muslim women supported by American, Canadian, and other feminists.

Furthermore, they write articles in support of Islam. They believe that Islam protects women and that Islam by nature is pro-women. This is a naïve belief, but what is its origin?

Gabby Aossey, a feminist author, offers us a strange interpretation of the attitude of Islam toward women. In her opinion, Western feminism (as she calls it) is far from true feminism. *Real feminism can be found only in Islam because only there women are appropriately treated.* But what does she mean?

In one of her articles, Aossey declares: “If we want to be respected as women and taken seriously in all our endeavors we should look to a new source; Muslim women” (Aossey par. 2). Why should we do it? Because, as she goes on, “Muslim women, as well as Muslim men, see every body as a sacred temple, especially the female body. Opposed to exposing themselves, it is through modesty. When we think of modern feminists we should stray away from the new American trends" (Aossey par. 2). *Ergo*, America is terrible, but Islam is salutary.

However, her reader can object: Islam does wrong to women. Aossey repudiates this assertion and writes that "Islam has a culture and history of women empowerment. In the Qur'an, which is believed to be God's word told to Prophet Muhammad, women and men are described as equals in everyday actions and responsibilities" (Aossey par. 3). She explains that the wife of the prophet Muhammad has been treated with respect by all Muslims, and she is one of the ideals of a woman and a model for womanhood.[8] Aossey goes on, "When it comes to family, charity, children, sex, and much more, a man and a woman have the same duties and that is to continue on the straight path" (Aossey par. 3).

Indeed, some Muslim women have impacted the history of humanity- for instance, the mothers of the Ottoman sultans were significant figures in the past. However, we can compare them to their Western counterparts, and we will see that England, Spain, and other European countries provided women with much more power in the past. However, what about normal women who do not belong to the class of Muslim noblemen (or the elite in Muslim societies)?

The author claims that these women are not forced to do anything; they freely accept all regulations existing in Muslim societies. Contrary to the common conviction, the *hijab is a symbol of women empowerment and their free will.* As Aossey states,

---

[8] The Prophet had at least eleven wives; some scholars say as many as thirteen. Others report that he had a total of twenty-three wives, but that he did not consummate marriages with nine of these spouses, which puts the total amount of legitimate wives at fourteen. At least one was betrothed to him at nine years old. Only Khadija and Maria bore him children.

"Hijab is the headscarf that is worn by Muslim woman and no; it is not supposed to be forced on them by their fathers and husbands. Wearing or not wearing the Hijab reflects a Muslim woman's own a personal choice" (Aossey par. 5).

Here we arrive at the absurdity of Western feminists defending the wearing of the hijab. What is the hijab in reality? We should answer this question by referring to the purpose of wearing it. Married women must wear it to show that they are married and that no one can look at them. The idea is simple: the woman has her hijab (or burqa, depending on the particular country); no one can look at her; therefore, no one can try to tempt her. In such a way, she will remain loyal to her husband. If she does not wear her hijab, then she "says" that she is single and everyone can ask for her hand.

Yes, all this looks wonderful, but this is only the official explanation of this "rule." In what a way does a woman say "yes" to an unknown man if she does not wear a hijab? Where is the respect for her personality? Why should her clothing decide for how she is to be treated by men? Furthermore, *why do women have to wear hijab? Why don't their husbands wear a covering as well? In what way are men's faces different from women's faces*? Where are the equal duties about which Aossiy writes?

The explanation is obvious. Married women are forced to believe that the hijab is their "guardian," It is the only thing that grants them some rights. Without the hijab, they practically lose all their rights and can be harassed by unknown men. Hence, the hijab is what gives them rights and privileges; losing it deprives them of such rights. Where is the logic here?

The feminist author quoted here says that it is nice for women to cover their heads and not to be proud of their physical attractiveness. Beauty is inside us, she writes.

Muslim women teach us that we have to be more modest and not to evaluate people according to their physical appearance. This is OK, but she goes on by writing the following: "We have been conditioned to think that American women are the free and that Muslim women are the suppressed, but this is twisted to me. I finally understood who is really oppressed by a patriarchal society and it is us" (Aossey par. 6). Of course, she refers here to radical feminist movements which fight for more "sexual liberty." This is Free the Nipplers movement. Aossey says that Muslim women should be treated with more respect than the representatives of this movement: "Woman who wear hijab have freed themselves from a man's and a society's judgmental gaze; the Free the Nipplers have not" (Aossey par. 6).

This view is quite controversial. Yes, there is a lot of fornication nowadays; but this is not the same as individual liberty. People have rights, and they choose what to do with them. They choose what type of behavior to adhere to. Some can be modest; others can be fornicators. Nevertheless, all of this cannot lead to legal punishment. The hijab is the opposite- women without the hijab can even be sentenced and go to prison! They do not have any options to choose from.

In brief, here we witness a manipulation: *American values are attacked and replaced with Islamic values*. How is this done? By referring to a particular (we can call it sectarian) movement which is not really popular in America. Some women support the Free the Nipplers movement, but the majority of women do not.

The author's only aim is to prove that Islam stands far above Christianity, on which Western society is founded. It would be serious trouble for the Christian who takes the aforementioned view literally. Christianity never claimed that women should remain in a veil and be "hidden" from all men they do not know personally. It has only maintained the moral ideal of the honest and loyal woman taking care of her family beside her husband. Islam, as we can see, does not put the wife next to her husband. *How can they have equal rights and duties if men are allowed to have four wives? Where is the love between the spouses*? Aossey could even defend polygamy if she wants so. She can say that polygamy is suitable for women and that it helps them look after children better. Alternatively, Islam defends women; hence they should accept everything as a gift from God.

The truth is unfortunate, and this is not an islamophobic assertion. Islam does not feel comfortable with the idea to give freedom to women. It cannot allow them to do whatever they want. It regulates their lives from birth to death. Regarding the behavior and way of living of men, it is much more relaxed. *The hijab is a symbol of male domination and marginalization of women in Muslim societies. Women are made to believe that this is their own choice; that by wearing the hijab or the burqa, they will gain respect and higher social status*. They are not aware that this "decision" is enforced on them from external forces.

Now, what is the stance of feminism toward such naïve media articles? There is some support for authors such as Aossey. Generally, contemporary feminists refrain from criticizing Islam, and in some cases, they even use it as a "weapon" for attacking the "Western patriarchy"! Their marches for women rights can also include Muslim women, and the latter wear their hijabs as a symbol of "emancipation."

Here we will turn to Julie Bindel, one of the few feminists who are challenging the narrative of the "women-friendly Islam." In her article "Why Are So Many Left-wing Progressives Silent About Islam's Totalitarian Tendencies?", she writes the following: "I am appalled at so-called progressives that capitulate to Islamist men, and make an exception for Islam as a religion…What is behind this hypocrisy? From where I am standing it is simple: the fear of being labelled 'Islamophobic'" (Bindel, UnHerd par. 1). In short, if someone calls Islam misogynic, he/she will be attacked as a "racist," "nationalist," or an "Islamophobe." Islam cannot be criticized; it should be admired.

The result of all this is that in present Britain, Muslim courts appear, and they are even protected by the existing legal system there. Leftists are affiliated with defending the rights of Muslims; hence they feel that they must support Islam in all of its aspects, including wearing the hijab. However, the consequences of this could be dangerous: "People afraid of being called Islamophobes have created space for hardline Muslim men to promote sharia courts, the wearing of the full-face veil, arranged marriage, female genital mutilation (FGM), and gender segregation in public places" (Bindel, UnHerd par. 4). This is a manipulated fear, which aims at making Muslim men more powerful in their societies. They are left to make their own legislation, which is an alternative legislation in Britain. As a secular country, the United Kingdom cannot allow such practices; but in reality, it does.

As Bindel points out, she tried to investigate how these sharia courts appeared in Britain without being banned and persecuted with legal means. In 2014 she published an investigation into the disappearance of a teenage girl, Charlene Downes, and the website *Islamophobia Watch* added the name of Bindel to their blacklist. As she explains,

"I was told by a number of men, and some feminists, that by exposing the grooming gang phenomenon I was, in the words of one 'anti-racist feminist' that I was playing into the hands of the BNP (British National Party)" (Bindel UnHerd, par. 12). This is nothing but manipulation. One cannot criticize Islam because he/she will be seen as a "racist." This is not the proper attitude toward criticizing Islam. Moreover, as Bindel observes, Christianity and Judaism have been criticized by these very feminists. She remarks that "Islam is somehow given a free pass by the very progressives that would not think twice about marching through London to protest the Pope's visit, or expressing outrage at orthodox Jewish men refusing to sit next to women on flights" (Bindel, UnHerd par. 17).

About this hypocrisy, nothing else can be said but that it is unfair to Christianity. *Christianity has been much more open toward other religions in general, and this cannot be seen in Islam*. There is no tolerance in Islam for other religions. There is no tolerance even within Muslim communities in Christian countries. Nevertheless, feminists, on the contrary, say that critics of Islam are "racists." As Bindel points out, there was a controversy related to wearing the hijab or burqa in public institutions in France. Some feminists were against wearing it, and consequently were criticized from their Leftist fellows: "Even some renowned 'old school' feminists have bought into the notion that criticising Islam is racist. Christine Delphy, the renowned feminist intellectual, has also criticised feminists in France, including refugees from Iran that support the ban on the veil" (Bindel, UnHerd par. 16).

This is the most absurd thing: women from Iran, who emigrated to Britain or France, are criticized because they tell the truth about the antagonistic and misogynistic attitude of Islam toward women! These women, born in Muslim countries, are accused of being anti-Muslims.

In another article regarding Islam, Bindel discusses precisely the problem of sharia courts in Britain. This is one of the articles that made her a target of ideological attacks by pro-Islam feminists. In "Muslim Women Deserve Better Than Sharia Law," she discusses the recently established sharia courts in the United Kingdom, especially in England. The British police have ignored these courts, perhaps because the attitude of the majority of politicians is not negative. These courts violate the secular character of the British state, thereby leading to the question who and how has allowed them to emerge.

In guidelines published by an organization defending sharia law in Britain, some shocking ideas are found. These guidelines "…penalise widows, non-believers and children born outside marriage. Illegitimate and adopted children are not sharia heirs. The male heirs in most cases receive double the amount inherited by a female heir of the same class. Non-Muslims may not inherit at all" (Bindel, Standpoint par. 4). Additionally, only Muslim marriages are considered legal! All this takes place in one of the most secular countries globally, where all religions are officially held equal before the law.

The scandal related to sharia courts began in 2008 when one of the so-called Muslim Arbitration Tribunal leaders ruled that the offenders in six cases of violence against women were not to be punished. He decided to "advise the men to take anger management classes and receive mentoring from so-called community elders so that marriages could be 'saved'" (Bindel, Standpoint par. 8). No doubt, this "ruling" only protects the interests of the men involved. This is entirely against the law, but sharia law has a different interpretation of what is domestic violence. In theory, it condemns it; but in reality, violence within marriages is not punished. The worst thing is that the British police are never informed of this; thus, they never intervene.

The reason for all this passivity of the authorities is that they are careful in investigating violence committed by Muslims. This is an unofficial policy of the British police regarding Muslim communities. There is a silent approval of the existence of sharia courts. This fact makes some Muslims in Britain angry with the state. Not all Muslims support sharia law. As Bindel points out, “Many British Muslims are critical of the British establishment’s support for sharia. Tehmina Kazi, director of British Muslims for Secular Democracy, says sharia councils should be penalised when they try to assume a legal status that they do not have” (Bindel, Standpoint par. 17). Especially Muslim women are subjected to two types of violence: physical violence at home, and legal violence from these sharia courts. Even if they want a divorce, it is rarely granted to them. Divorce is not seen in the same way in which secular societies do. For sharia courts, divorce should be avoided at any possible cost, even if the woman in question is subjected to terrible violence (including rape). Women are “advised” to not turn to the police in cases of domestic violence. They agree because the Muslim community is the only thing which could help them and protect them.

Some Muslim women are unemployed and do not speak English. They are also indoctrinated as to believe that men are always right and that beating is not violence. These women are utterly dependent upon their husbands and/or parents. The only way to help them is when someone intervenes from without. However, this rarely happens because all these acts of violence are known only within the given community.

The proponents of sharia courts refer to what Aossey calls "free choice" of women. Women have decided themselves to adhere to sharia courts, so these rulings are legal, it is said. Here we see the absurdity of the views of Aossey who was quoted earlier in this subchapter. If they freely choose the hijab, can we say that the acts of violence are also chosen by them? Moreover, some women even believe that they are guilty for life because someone manipulates them. Where is the end of all this? There should be an objective borderline between what the law says and what one believes. As Bindel puts it, "Just because some Muslim women argue that they should be allowed access to the sharia system does not mean we should let it become a part of British law." She goes on with the following example "Habiba Jaan is the founder of Aurat, a support service for Muslim women in the West Midlands. She told me that only a decade ago she rarely heard of sharia courts, but now 'they appear to be on every doorstep'" (Bindel, Standpoint par. 20).

Feminism must intervene because the rights of Muslim women are regularly violated in their communities. This is the task of all Western feminists. Instead of arguing in favor of domestic violence by calling it "free choice of women," they must think more of the consequences of their actions. Things will change for the worse if no one does anything. Such feminists are responsible for the violence taking place among Muslims precisely because of the former's silence. As Julie Bindel observes, "It seems incredible that after more than four decades of feminism in the West so many on the Left are willing to sacrifice women's rights, in particular the rights of Muslim-born women, in the name of so-called religious freedom" (Bindel, Standpoint par. 18).

Bindel, however, does not realize that the problem lies in the general attitude of the Leftists. It is not merely about a mistake or a misinterpretation. The problem is the very insistence on tolerance. Feminism has become a political movement that tries to direct the foreign policy of the United States or Britain. Feminism should deal only with a narrow range of issues- women's rights, discrimination, violence against women. Instead, it has gone as far as to speak about climate change, the wars in the Middle East, globalization, poverty, racism, and so forth. However, feminists nowadays are competent in all possible spheres of life- they know a lot about religion, science, morality, foreign affairs. They amalgamate Humanities, Social sciences and biology. When they want, they deal with biology; otherwise, they direct their attention to sociology. This is wrong, and because of this, sharia courts have emerged in Western countries. This cannot be allowed to happen in the United States, and feminists should be aware of that. Authors such as Aossey would be used as tools to defend the enforcing of the antihuman legislation known as sharia law.

The position of Bindel could appear controversial for the Christian reader. She is known as a representative of lesbian feminism, which claims that women should enter romantic relationships with women only. But here we have presented her views regarding the monstrousness of the sharia law. She is one of the few feminists, as we said, who tried to react against sharia law and the increasing influence of pro-Islamic organizations. As this case shows, contemporary feminists are not thoroughgoing and do not care about their doctrine's consistency. Furthermore, this shows also their inability to understand political processes around the world. It is better for feminists not to be engaged with foreign affairs (for example, many of them now are supporting the Kurds only because of the female soldiers there).

Feminism is not compatible with Islam due to the fact that Islam is anti-women at its core. It is a worldview which marginalizes women in a way much worse than medieval society.

3.3 Feminism against femininity. Feminism against women

Summary:

Is feminism antifeminine? Are feminists masculine? Here we will attempt to find the answers to these questions. It will also be shown that feminism, in its contemporary version, does a lot of harm to femininity and to women in general.

We already touched upon the question of whether feminists should be "real women." Moreover, what is a "real woman" in general? In France, we noticed that feminism is much more "feminine," and feminism is not considered entirely masculine. Women do not need to become men in order to be independent. Nevertheless, in the United States and Britain, things are different- as one can see, contemporary feminists are far from the romantic ideal of a woman.

The initial idea was that women should be more independent and should have more rights. However, over time, feminism has changed. It began emphasizing physical and spiritual strength; it rejected the need to have family and children. Thus, the emancipated woman is seen a having a career, without a family. She behaves like a man-she needs to earn more and more money, and all her plans revolve around this aim. Tenderness, caring, and love are not seen as her personal traits anymore. This woman should be even brutal if this is needed. Is she a woman, or is she rather a man, or is this gender dysphoria?

Karlyn Campbell discusses this issue in her article "Femininity and Feminism: To be or Not to be a Woman." She finds the root of the problem in an opposition between the concepts of womanhood and personhood. Women's rights are defended in a universalist way, i.e. as natural rights of all human beings. Although, this defense does not take into account the unique character of women. It looks like feminism endorses women's rights as equal and similar to men's rights. She finds an ideological problem here and says that it is "a conflict posed by the concept of 'womanhood' or 'femininity' on the one hand, and personhood on the other, a conflict that has its roots in the origins of feminism" (Campbell 101). When it is emphasized on the concept of womanhood, then the notion of a person disappears. For example, many critics of the first-wave feminism stated that women need to stay at home and look after children because they look more feminine in this way. Women should work more on their beauty than on their intelligence and education. These were the arguments of the people refuting feminism and claiming that women have everything they need. Campbell understands this as a choice: a woman is either a woman or a person. Thus, feminism took the way to personhood. This is all due to the fact that "the concept of woman, with its negation of personhood, is the basis for sisterhood and the precondition for a feminist movement, yet it is just this concept which must be destroyed" (Campbell 103).

Strangely enough, lesbian feminism comprehends the ideal woman as feminine. As Campbell observes, the proponents of lesbian feminism "cherish what is feminine in contrast to what is masculine, defined as patriarchal and phallocentric…the goal of such feminism is the woman-identified woman who withdraws from the masculine culture, which is characterized by rape, genocide, and war" (Campbell 104). Nevertheless, they are an exception: most feminists prefer to see women as having traits typical of men-aggression, rivalry, progressing in their career, thinking more about money than about children, and so forth.

Do feminist women possess traits which are seen as masculine? Are these feminists masculine? Here we do not ask whether they are women: this is obvious. However, men can be more feminine than others, and women can be more masculine than other women. G. Madison discusses this problem, U. Aasa, J. Wallert, and M. A. Woodley in their article "Feminist Activist Women are Masculinized in Terms of Digit-ratio and Social Dominance: A Possible Explanation for the Feminist Paradox" (2014). These researchers conducted a survey based on the assumption that women-feminists are physiologically and biologically "more masculine" than non-feminist women. The researchers refer to a strange phenomenon which is called a feminist paradox. It reads as follows: "Three-quarters of women are concerned about women's rights while less than one-third consider themselves feminist" (Madison et al. 1). What is the reason why only a small number of women support feminism? If feminism defends their rights and is ultimately pro-women, why only about 25 % of women and even less (depending on the country) take the stance of feminism?

The researcher team assumes the following: "Part of the explanation for this paradox might result from the fact that there are many different conceptions of what feminism is or ought to be, and that it lacks a commonly established definition" (Madison et al. 1). Some women believe that feminism is only radical feminism and does not bring anything good to women (in general). Perhaps feminism today has gone too far, and many women do not want to identify themselves with it.

Madison and her fellow researchers have worked on this issue. According to them, the fact that feminism is diverse cannot explain the feminist paradox. There must be something else. As they put it, "The feminist paradox, or the dissociation between feminist self-identification and belief in equality, and the alleged misrepresentation in the media all suggest an underlying inconsistency or conflict" (Madison et al. 2). Their assumption is that feminist activists (so they focus entirely on political activism) are more masculine, and probably this makes some women refrain from joining such organizations or political parties. The thesis formulated by the team is the following: "The activists who shape feminist attitudes and beliefs are themselves generally more physiologically and psychologically masculinized than is typical for women" (Madison et al. 3). As their survey conducted by these researchers in Sweden during a feminist conference shows, they have more masculine features (for example, assertiveness) than other women.

We will not present any details of this survey because the reader could analyze it personally. The data presented by the researchers demonstrate that these feminist activists behave and think more like men than women. Of course, it can be objected that this conclusion is too general, that it cannot be applied to all cases of feminism. Not all feminists in the world are masculine or "think like men." Madison and her research team declare that this objection is correct: “It would therefore be logically incorrect to infer that, for example, all feminist activists are masculinized or that all groups that are more masculinized are also feminist activists” (Madison et al. 8).

Feminism itself does not indicate that its proponents must be masculine. On the other hand, *there is a clear tendency of masculinization*, and contemporary feminists should reflect more on that if they want to attract more members to their organizations. If feminism continues to be so isolated from reality and the real needs of women, it will become a dogmatic worldview endorsed by a remote community of masculinized women.

Another objection, however, can be directed against the conclusion mentioned above. How can we be sure that “masculine” and “feminine” features are real? Are they objective, or are they dependent on our thought? Are they “social constructs”?

In the past (before the 20th century) it was thought that some features are not typical of women. We already mentioned that the first feminists fought against this prejudice- that women are not intelligent enough, that they cannot think practically, that women are too emotional, that women should deal only with love and the family. This is an example of a wrong stereotype about women’s personality. Nevertheless, feminism today says that all other features which are ascribed to women are social constructs, that they are not objective, and that men can also possess them. Such features include: tenderness, lovingness, care, better verbal skills (women speak much more and have richer vocabulary), less physical aggression, too much care about their physical appearance, and others. As one can see, some men can possess all these features, which does not mean that they are women. However, generally, most women have these features, and this fact has biological roots. It is related to the fact that women become pregnant, give birth, and then look after children. Women should be more caring and tender; otherwise, they will not be able to look after children properly.

Men, on the other hand, have been more aggressive because of different factors. Nonetheless, a careful study of the contemporary situation of men will show that with the rise of modern civilization, interpersonal physical aggression has decreased. Hence, we cannot assert that men are aggressive, but rather that they are more aggressive than women. These are two different statements. The first one says that a certain feature is absolute; the second says that this feature is relative; it exists in relation to women.

Indeed, it is not correct to claim that all men have only masculine traits and that women cannot possess these traits. What could be said about driving skills? In the past, it was believed that women could not drive; but now we see that many women are drivers. Therefore, some skills can be improved depending on the situation. Likewise, women could also be good soldiers if trained properly (as the case with Israel shows- there is mandatory service for women). Moreover, the reverse is true: men can be excellent parents and caregivers. However, there are things which cannot be changed: men cannot breastfeed; they cannot give birth. This makes their attitude and relation with children different from women.

All this does not mean that masculinity and femininity are not objective. They are, but they have "hard essence" and "soft essence." The soft essence can change over time, depending on the place, time, and given culture. The hard essence- the fact that men are stronger physically and that only women can breastfeed- is not subject to changes. This depends on human biology, not on social or cultural conventions.

To be sure, some men can be more masculine than other men, in the sense of physical strength, decisiveness and lack of tenderness. This does not mean that the other men are women or that they are not "real men." The differences between individual males are not as significant as between men and women. The differences between the sexes remain prominent, and the gap cannot be overcome unless one decides to eliminate human biology from the analysis.

As we noted already, it is not correct to think that the meaning of life of women is to be beautiful. The meaning of life of both men and women should be the same because all of us are humans. Our mission in life is to love and create in all possible ways. It is not fair to deny men the possibility to love because "men should be strong, and love makes them weak." Nevertheless, the ways men and women express their love are different- this is indisputable. Women are much more expressive, i.e., they like speaking about their feelings. Is this a social construct or a stereotype?

To some extent, it is, because different cultures have a different understanding of how a woman should express her feelings. However, generally, women are more emotional (or more expressive) than men. So this fact again confirms our conclusion: that masculinity and femininity are objective, although they exist in a mutually dependent relation with each other.

Another paradox related to feminism and femininity is that women, although having gained independence in recent decades, still feel unhappy. In an article by Lynne Marie Kohm; Diane Chandler, and Doris Gomez, "Christianity, Feminism, and the Paradox of Female Happiness," it is asserted that feminism itself cannot bring happiness, and there are many reasons for this. A report from 2009 referred by them "documented some surprising facts. Since 1970 women's self-reported happiness has fallen, relative to that of men, according to the study. This seems paradoxical, given the tremendous strides made by the women's movement" (Kohm et al. 1). According to the authors, this results from the rise of the materialist worldview and the decreasing power of Christianity. Kohm and her fellows assert that "feminists and women leaders ought to seriously consider the Christian foundations of any claim to gender equality and the resulting implications of personal faith upon genuine happiness and personal fulfillment" (Kohm et al. 2).

Modern feminism had done much harm to women and their cause because it has moved away from its initial goals and moral principles. By emphasizing the idea that women should be similar to men and behave like men, feminists have turned to the conception of the masculine woman. This is what women cannot accept and do not want to adhere to.

One of the examples of this is contraception. The latter was invented as a means for birth control. It was meant to help women advance in their careers instead of looking after children. Simultaneously, it has made women more vulnerable and men more irresponsible because birth control has helped men objectify women as objects of pleasure. As they observe, "the advent of contraception brought with it a major shift in reproductive responsibility away from men, and in many cases, completely on women, clearly a move away from gender equality." The same can be said about abortion, which "often serves to release men completely from responsibility, another dramatic move away from gender equality" (Kohm et al. 26). Ironically enough, all this has ensued in unhappy women who have to carry the burden of their career and family life. As the researchers claim, “Reproductive freedom has led to dramatic harm to women, and dramatic benefits to men” (Kohm et al. 27).

All this happens because no one takes into account the relations between persons, and especially between men and women. *Feminism has always thought about women without trying to involve men. By insisting on more freedom for women, it has forgotten that men will take on more and more burdens*. Moreover, men are right in refusing to do so- Why should they take on all of these burdens if no one has asked them before what they think?

Particularly abortion on demand is considered part of the “sexual liberty” enjoyed nowadays. But it is not liberty. It is a way in which men might control women. A woman alone cannot easily pass through pregnancy and give birth. She needs the assistance of her relatives and friends. Thus, it happens that in the majority of cases, women do what their partners or husbands want. This is not freedom but rather dependency.

Another thing to be noted in connection with the problem of birth control is that this approach sexualizes women; instead of perceiving them as persons, it says that they are sexual objects, and this is normal. As Kohm and her fellows maintain, “In many ways feminist philosophy, in its attempts to eradicate women from being defined by sexual, reproductive, and service abilities has allowed gender equality to be consumed, even cannibalized by those efforts” (Kohm et al. 44). *By saying that women can do anything with their bodies, it has identified them precisely with their bodies* and nothing else. By allowing “free choice” and the “my body is my choice” principle, feminism has actually turned women into sexual objects.

The involvement of feminists in problems related to homosexuals and lesbians has added another obstacle to achieving its goals. Kohm and her team remark that “this new emphasis on sexual orientation served to move the women’s rights movement further away from gender equality concerns.” The result of this process is “women’s rights and feminist philosophy being largely employed, even co-opted by lesbianism, for completely different issues such as same sex unions and assisted reproduction” (Kohm et al. 29). These issues are not merely different, but they even do more harm to women- by convincing some of them that children can be “produced” as in a factory and that this is easy and does not take any effort.

Additionally, they say the following about lesbianism: “Serving to separate, disconnect and disengage women and men, it has further deepened the gender chasm, and destroyed the liberal feminist movement from within” (Kohm et al. 29). Initially, feminism wanted to achieve harmony between men and women. But now, under the form of lesbianism, it already showed its aim to destroy marriages and the family and to propagate unnatural civil unions. By adding the weird ideas of Shulamith Firestone, who even proposes small children to get married, we can say that feminism today is a perverse principle formulated as a philosophy. Where is gender equality here? Where is the promised protection of women’s rights? How can women be sure that feminism is not controlled and managed by men? This is a reliable hypothesis given all the harm which has been done by feminism. As the authors conclude, “most women are uncomfortable with the total package offered by feminist philosophy, and some have embraced its successes without discarding their values of faith and family” (Kohm et al. 46).

Feminism has underestimated femininity and womanhood. It needs to go back to its roots- to the movement for the defense of women's rights. *Feminism should not be turned into a political party, ideology, or a worldview. This is not its mission. Feminism should protect women.*

Furthermore, women today do not feel protected by it; they feel abandoned by feminism. Their real needs are different from what contemporary feminism offers. Women need love, respect, harmony; not political struggles and empty promises.

Kohm and her research fellows conclude that *by turning to Christianity, feminism could regain some respect and could do a lot for the women in the world.* As they write, "Jesus valued women far above than afforded them by patriarchal society." He knew that "when women were defined exclusively in terms of their sexual, reproductive, and servant abilities they are stripped of their uniqueness and complexity as individuals created in the image and likeness of God" (Kohm et al. 44). Christianity and Christian values are missing in this worldview. Feminism without them will remain futile and without effect.

3.4 Conclusion

Feminism has turned into an ideology. This process cannot be traced back but is foundationless. There was a point in time when feminism ceased to be simply a movement for women's rights. We cannot say when and where, but this happened in reality. As Karlyn Campbell says, feminism is a rhetorical movement (that is, the discursive core of a social movement). It is driven by an ideological conflict, which is described by Campbell as follows: "An ideological conflict between the concepts of 'womanhood' and 'personhood' and by the rhetorical strategies summed up by the term 'consciousness raising' (Campbell 101). What should women do- should they become men or masculine? Should they cease to be women? What should an independent woman look like? Feminism depicts a strange picture of a world inhabited by masculine women, with great ambitions and plans and deprived of sensitivity. In its attempt to transform society, it has led to many absurdities, as shown in this chapter. It has stood against the family, against marriage and romantic relationships between men and women (since these are also used by men to control women); it has declared itself in favor of Islam with its dangerous anti-women practices. Because feminists usually try to identify themselves with the Left, they blindly adhere to the ideology of Leftism and do not dare express their skepticism regarding certain points in this ideology. To all this, we can add the materialist worldview and atheism, which makes of feminism what it is today: a worldview without stable basis, without real hope and faith, and without love and tenderness. This is a cold world consisting of cold relationships. This is a world where only money and wealth are important; feelings and relations do not matter here.

However, is there any alternative to feminism? Perhaps we can find such one. What should we say about Christianity? What is its attitude toward women? What does it say regarding women's rights? What does it say about the family and community? Let us see in the following chapter.

Chapter IV: Christianity and women

By now, we have analyzed the central points of the feminist ideology. We discussed the history of feminism, the core of radical feminism, and some paradoxes and contradictions found in contemporary feminism. However, we also know that feminists attack religion, and especially Christianity, perceiving it as "anti-women." Here we will deal with this issue. First, we will turn to the conception that Judeo-Christian religions have replaced the cult of the Goddess with the worship of a "male deity." Then we will analyze what the proper stance of Christianity toward women is. To do this, we also need to interpret some passages from the Holy Bible, and we will also interpret the role and mission of the Blessed Virgin Mary, the Mother of God.

4.1 Ancient cults of the Goddess and their alleged suppression by Christianity

Summary:

The conception of the ancient "female religion" will be discussed here. According to Merlin Stone, these ancient cults of the Great Goddess were destroyed later by the so-called "northern invaders" in order to justify the rule of men as kings. We will discuss this conception besides the views of Andrea Dworkin. We will refer to some passages from the Holy Bible to show whether these accusations are justified.

Christianity never said that God is a "male deity" or a "man."[9] It is not characteristic of Christian theology to describe God in terms of masculinity. This is seen as part of earthly existence. God cannot have any gender. However, some feminists claim that the Christian conception of God depicts Him as a "man." This, according to them, is rooted in the patriarchal society, which is based on the postulate that men stand higher than women. Here we will discuss this hypothesis. As the reader will see, there is some truth in the claim that in ancient times, there were many cults of the Goddess, and that ancient and pre-ancient societies had a different understanding of the role of women.

First, we will turn to some ideas exposed by Andrea Dworkin. She asserts that Christianity is misogynic, that it is based on hatred toward women. In her opinion, "The Christians in their manifold variety were continuing the highly developed Jewish tradition of misogyny, patriarchy, and sexist suppression, alternatively known as the Garden-of-Eden-Hype" (Dworkin 137). As we will see later when we will discuss Merlin Stone's work on the cult of the Goddess, ancient Israelites initiated this practice of repression of the "female religions." Dworkin says that their myth of Original Sin was an attack on women and femininity. As she puts it, "Adam's legacy post-Eden is sexual knowledge, mortality, guilt, toil, and the fear of castration. Adam became a human male, the head of a family. His sin was lesser than Eve's, seemingly by definition again" (Dworkin 138). Original Sin with all its consequences is to be put on Eve, on the woman. Adam was not wise enough to oppose her decision, but this is because women are temptresses, and he was tempted; he was unable to think rationally and wisely. This way of thinking, Dworkin says, can be found in other religions, not only in the Judeo-

[9] Jesus, the Second Person of the Most Holy Trinity is fully God and fully man.

Christian tradition. In Taoism, the feminine is opposed to the masculine. The feminine has all negative characteristics of which one can think: “The Chinese ontology…describes cosmic movement as cyclical, thoroughly interwoven manifestation of yang (masculine, aggressive, light, spring, summer) and yin (female, passive, dark, fall, winter)” (Dworkin 164). Therefore, in Taoism, the feminine is defined not in itself, but only in relation to the masculine. All positive phenomena and entities are seen as masculine. This does not mean that only men possess them; however, this is a reflection of the mentality of the Chinese at that time.

The negative perception of the feminine could only lead to disasters. What is more, this actually took place in the Middle Ages when some women were persecuted as “witches.” For example, in the book *Malleus Maleficarum,* the woman is defined in an eldritch way. As Dworkin exposes it, the woman is defined in terms of carnality. Women are defined as evil and capable to do anything bad. She analyzes this work as based on the fear of women and that which is feminine: “We are dealing with an existential terror of women, of the ‘mouth of the womb,’ stemming from a primal anxiety about male potency, tied to a desire for self (phallic) control; men have deep-rooted castration fears which are expressed as a horror of the womb” (Dworkin 134). This fear comes from the difficulty to understand pregnancy and the act of giving birth.

This interpretation may be wrong, but the witch hunts in the Middle Ages were indeed a tragic event. It is hard to estimate how many women died because of them, but its basis was wrong. Indeed, feminism today uses this disaster to attack Christianity and to demonstrate that the Catholic Church has always had a bad attitude toward women. Nevertheless, the witch hunt was not planned by the Church itself; it was instead a result of the personal ambitions of people outside the Church. Like the Crusades, it should be comprehended as a deviation from the Church's teaching, not as its demonstration and application.

Andrea Dworkin contrasts this alleged Christian attitude to the worldview existing prior to Judeo-Christian religions. She is convinced that primitive religions showed more respect toward femininity and that they even thought of humans as androgynous. As she asserts, "The original myths all concern a primal androgyne —an androgynous godhead, an androgynous people." The disappearance of these myths was not by accident, as she observes: "The corruptions of these myths of a primal androgyne without exception uphold patriarchal notions of sexual polarity, duality, male and female as opposite and antagonistic" (Dworkin 162). What can we find about this disappearance?

She finds some remnants of the pre-ancient myths in Indian religions. For instance, "There are still devotional religious practices which harken back to the mythology of the primal androgyne- Tantra, for instance, in both its Tibetan and Indian manifestations, clearly participates in that tradition" (Dworkin 170). This is a fact- Tantrism contains some elements of the idea that the difference between masculine and feminine is rather an illusion, and that initially, they existed as one whole. Nevertheless, in Hinduism and Buddhism- the most important religions which were born in India- there is no such conception. Hence, Dworkin should say that these two religions also suppressed the myth of the "primal androgyne."

The ideas of Dworkin were actually borrowed from Merlin Stone's book *When God Was a Woman.* Stone's work is not the first one that discussed the problem of the cults of the Goddess; nonetheless, it is the first work which took this issue in the context of feminism.

Now we turn to Merlin Stone's conception. Stone asks many questions concerning women and religion. Two of them are the following: "What had life been like for women who lived in a society that venerated a wise and valiant female Creator? Why had the members of the later male religions fought so aggressively to suppress that earlier worship—even the very memory of it?" (Stone xiii). Her book is an attempt to give answers to these queries. It is important to note that her position is not as radical as Dworkin's views.

Her explanation is that these pre-ancient cults were intentionally suppressed. We do not know precisely by whom, but we know that the Holy Bible is the product of this process. Merlin Stone claims that "The writers of the Judeo-Christian Bible, as we know it, seem to have purposely glossed over the sexual identity of the female deity who was held sacred by the neighbors of the Hebrews in Canaan, Babylon and Egypt" (Stone xviii). Hence, in the Holy Bible, we can find some information about these cults.

How did all this take place and why? What was this pre-ancient society? As the author explains, "Sir James Frazer believed that the high status of women was initially responsible for the veneration and esteem of the female deity. He cited the Pelew clan of Micronesia, where the women were considered to be socially and politically superior to the men" (Stone 31). At that time, the organization of societies were reflected in their pagan religions, which were centered on the Goddess. Of course, this was not their only deity. They had many deities, and there were many myths regarding them.

There are plenty of proofs for the existence of the Goddess on different continents. Some of the oldest pieces of art found in Europe are dedicated to the Goddess. Egypt, Sumer, Babylon, and even ancient Greece (in its earliest stages) had such cults. As Stone states, "The Great Goddess—the Divine Ancestress —had been worshiped from the beginnings of the Neolithic periods of 7000 BC until the closing of the last Goddess temples, about AD 500" (Stone xii).

It is held that the cult of the female deity is related to the fertility of the land; perhaps the members of those societies did not understand the connection between sexual intercourse and children, as Stone suggests. Thus, women were perceived as mothers, and giving birth was seen as a miracle.

However, all of this had another consequence. The line of inheritance began with the mother, not with the father as it is now. Merlin Stone remarks that "A consciousness of the relationship of the veneration of the Goddess to the matrilineal descent of name, property and the rights to the throne is vital in understanding the suppression of the Goddess religion" (Stone 61). The so-called Northern invaders destroyed this cult, as she asserts. The question is, Why did they do it?

Perhaps one of the explanations is that these pre-ancient societies were agricultural, not nomadic. This way of living required all men and women to take part in the process of cultivation of plants and to take care of the crops. Thus, it was customary for them to worship fertility, which meant food and survival. Women were important actors in the process, and their role in society was seen as crucial. As Stone asserts, "In agreement with the generally accepted theory that women were responsible for the development of agriculture, as an extension of their food-gathering activities, there were female deities everywhere who were credited with this gift to civilization" (Stone 3).[10]

Men dealt with hunting, but this depended on the particular tribe and time. We cannot be sure that some women (especially before having children) did not participate in hunting. As Stone observes, the cults of the Goddess were related not only to fertility but also to hunting. In Greece, the goddess Artemis (in Rome it was Diana) was responsible for it. Another goddess- Athens- is famous as the virgin-warrior, also as a symbol of wisdom. In various mythologies, the author remarks, there are struggles between male and female deities, which shows that the latter were not entirely passive. Hence, if something changed, it was brought about by the new peoples and tribes that came from Asia- the Indo-Europeans, or Aryans.

The trouble, Stone says, is not simply in the subordination of women as a result of these waves of invaders. It is instead in the fact that these pre-ancient religions are forgotten, and no one wants to examine them properly. We do not need to have the same cults now, she admits; we simply need to complement our knowledge of religion with this knowledge, because female deities were crucial in this very distant past. This awareness and knowledge, she says, "may be used to cut through the many oppressive and falsely founded patriarchal images, stereotypes, customs and laws that were developed as direct reactions to Goddess worship by the leaders of the later male-worshiping religions" (Stone xxv). In short, if we all realized that female deities existed in the past, we would be more critical to Christianity as a product of a patriarchal society.

---

[10] Pertaining to agriculture, a disparity emerged among men and women circa the year 5,500 BC, with the commencement of millet harvesting. This ragbag grain was very difficult to cultivate and harvest, and the disproportion in strength between the sexes became pronounced and conspicuous. This distinction was not apparent prior in the demesne of farming.

The "northern invaders" came to Europe in several waves, from the beginning of the first millennium BC to 3rd-4th centuries AD. These invaders changed the worldview of the ancient nations in order to transform the structure of their societies. Stone writes that the availability of myths which say that a male deity created the world "strongly hints at the possibility that many of these myths were written by priests of the invading tribes to justify the supremacy of the new male deities and to justify the installation of a king as the result of the relationship of that king to the male deity" (Stone 67).

However, the Indo-European tribes invaded Europe about the time of Christ and even later. Thus, the concept of "northern invaders" is vague and not very accurate. This remains only Stone's hypothesis; at any rate, it is a fact that the ancient Israelites had different laws from the laws of their neighbors, which speaks in favor of the hypothesis that something changed suddenly. The laws of the Levites, she observes, were entirely anti-women, and they deprived women of any privileges, which they would have had under the rule of other tribes. All this was carried out as an attack on paganism and pagan cults. These were destroyed not only because they were pagan but also because of the feminine aspect in them. Stone claims that "Into the laws of the Levites was written the destruction of the worship of the Divine Ancestress, and with it the final destruction of the matrilineal system" (Stone 179).

The Israelite laws were fierce and did not give any rights to women. Women were not held to be autonomous beings with free will. This was due to Israelites' ambition to introduce the patrimonial line of inheritance. One of the shocking examples which can be found in these laws is the following: "So determined were the Levites that a reverent regard for the paternity of children be developed that among them even violent rape was equated with marriage, much as it was among the Indo- European-controlled Assyrians" (Stone 190). She goes on: "The rape of a virgin was honored as a declaration of ownership" (Stone 190). She then refers to Deuteronomy 22:28-29 where it is written that a man can have sexual intercourse with an unmarried woman and then claim her hand.[11] According to Stone's interpretation, this law allowed even for the rapist to marry the raped woman. Perhaps this is a misinterpretation, but it is certain that men had many more rights than women during this period, especially regarding marriage and divorce. At the same time, as she notes, some Israelites did not adhere to the laws: "The records of the Hebrew kings reveal that they kept large harems and most Hebrew men appear to have taken several wives" (Stone 191). Therefore, there was a contradiction between the laws and the reality, she concludes.

The Israelites' laws were stricter regarding women, as it is easy to be noticed. Stone writes that "The Levite laws of the Israelites, from the time of Moses onward, demanded virginity until marriage for all women, upon threat of death by stoning or burning, and, once married, total fidelity, only upon the part of the wife, also upon threat of death" (Stone 156). At the same time, virginity was not absolutely demanded from men. This law is proof that the father of every child had to be known with absolute certainty.

To be sure, these laws did not tolerate adultery from men as well. Women and men were punished in an identical way for adultery. However, women were punished more often than men.

---

[11] The context of Deuteronomy 22 demands the death of a rapist to purify the land. Also, in Exodus 22:17 stipulates that a woman does not have to marry the man who rapes her, but only has to honor her father and do what he says.

All these facts, however, speak only about the backwardness of that historical period. Merlin Stone goes further by claiming that the Holy Bible was written in such a way as to eradicate any trace of the "female religion;" with this, the Bible became a weapon against the rights of women. Stone does not precisely formulate this, but her reader (potentially) has this impression of her work.

Now let us address Original Sin as committed by Adam and Eve. According to Merlin Stone, this story was intentionally created to justify repressions against women in ancient Israelite society. Moreover, it can even be hypothesized that the story of Original Sin, at least as we know it, was fabricated later, and that[12] it did not exist initially. As Stone assumes, "the story which supposedly explained what happened at the very beginning of time, the image of woman as the dangerously seductive temptress, who brought about the fall of all humanity, may have been inserted" (Stone 197). In short, this story was not part of the Holy Bible, but someone inserted it intentionally to justify the brutal Levite laws.

Stone describes her own feelings regarding the story of Original Sin as something negative, which made her less confident in herself. This story in the way it is usually told makes women feel guilty, although they should be perceived as equal to men in this aspect. Medieval theology, she writes, puts too much stress on the guilt of women. Besides this, "I was also supposed to accept the idea that men, as symbolized by Adam, in order to prevent any further foolishness on my part, were presented with the right to

---

[12] In the Catholic Old Testament, three Books (Judith, Ruth and Esther) are named after Jewish women. Five women of the Hebrew Scriptures are defined as prophets: Miriam (Exodus 15:20), Deborah (Judges 4:4), Huldah (2 Kings 22:14), Noadiah (Nehemiah 6:14), and a "prophetess" (Isaiah 8:3). Three hundred thirtythree women are names in the Holy Bible; however, there are approximately two thousand eight hundred eightynine men named in the Holy Bible.

control me—to rule over me." Adam is wise, but Eve made him make a mistake- this is what the Bible teaches, Stone claims. She goes on by noting that "my penitent, submissive position as a female was firmly established by page three of the nearly one thousand pages of the Judeo-Christian Bible" (Stone 6).

Stone's remarks are not to be perceived as hostile to Christianity. She is right here in saying that deprivation of women of their rights was sometimes justified with this short passage from the Book of *Genesis*. It is not fair to speak of women as the guilty ones regarding Original Sin. Maybe in the past, there were some remarks of this kind, but today they are unacceptable. We can explain this attitude toward women with the social, political, and cultural context. The repressions against women are a historical fact; no one can disprove it. At the same time, we can assume that this was instead a misunderstanding of the Bible itself. This is due to the fact that humans are not perfect, and that they are disposed toward making mistakes. It is not fair and not justified to rely on the Bible when one wants to enslave other nations, all women, or whole groups of people. The story of Original Sin is perhaps to be seen metaphorically, not literally- this has been noted by many theologians (in accordance with the exegetical methods of the Early Church Fathers). Eve should not be seen as symbolizing all women, and the feminine in general. All of us are finite beings, and we commit sins because we are human beings. *The Bible does not teach that women are more susceptible to sin. If someone interprets the Bible in this way, then he/she is wrong*. Original Sin concerns all human beings, without any difference based on gender.

Another misunderstanding concerns the creation of human beings. Some people wrongly suggest that man was created first, and then woman (from his rib). This is again the result of the fact that the Bible is interpreted literally, instead of symbolically. Stone describes this wrong attitude as follows: "Man was created first. Woman was made for man. Only man was made in God's image. According to the Bible, and those who accepted it as the divine word, the male god favored men and had indeed designed them as naturally superior" (Stone 6).

The Catholic Church rejects this wrong stance toward women.[13] In the Catechism we read the following: "Man and woman are both with one and the same dignity 'in the image of God'. In their 'being-man' and 'being-woman', they reflect the Creator's wisdom and goodness" (Catechism 369). In a particular sense, man (male beings) is not the image of God simply because God is neither male nor female, as we already noted. The Catechism firmly states that "In no way is God in man's image. He is neither man nor woman. God is pure spirit in which there is no place for the difference between the sexes" (Catechism 370).

As the reader can see, Stone is not correct if we refer to the contemporary stance of the Church. She relates to old prejudices which have already disappeared. Christians today are taught that "Man and woman were made 'for each other' - not that God left them half-made and incomplete: he created them to be a communion of persons, in which each can be 'helpmate' to the other, for they are equal as persons" (Catechism 372).

All this, however, would not change Stone's point of view toward the Bible. She believes that the Bible itself is not God's work, but was written by a human hand in an

---

[13] The Blessed Virgin Mary is the Mother of God, the only perfect and sinless disciple of Her Son, Jesus. The Blessed Virgin is the only human who received the prevenient grace of Christ's Passion prior to its Consummation. Also, there are four women who are Doctors of the Church (Saints Catherine of Siena, Hildegard of Bingen, Teresa of Avila, and Therese of Lisieux). Also, there are thousands of women who have been canonized by the Holy Roman Catholic Church.

attempt to justify the existing laws at that time. The repression and persecution of the "female religion" took place because a new order in the society was needed in that epoch. Women had to become subordinated to men and deprived of many rights which they had before that moment. The "female religion" was attacked as immoral and "sexual."

However, this ancient religion was really "sexual," as Stone admits. She writes about the sexual rituals performed in the name of the Goddess: "In the worship of the female deity, sex was Her gift to humanity. It was sacred and holy…But in the religions of today we find an almost totally reversed attitude. Sex, especially non-marital sex, is considered to be somewhat naughty, dirty, even sinful" (Stone 154-5). Stone's hypothesis, as we mentioned earlier, is that the attack on this sexual practice was due not to moral reasons, but to political ambitions: "I suggest that it was upon the attempt to establish this certain knowledge of paternity, which would then make patrilineal reckoning possible, that these ancient sexual customs were finally denounced as wicked and depraved" (Stone 161). Ancient Israelite kings wanted to be certain about their heirs, and that no one else would have claims upon the throne. The eradication of ancient sexual rites meant that monogamy had to be introduced and maintained with all possible means. With this, the "female religion" ceased slowly to exist. As Stone assumes, "Its disappearance was gradually brought about, initially by the Indo-European invaders, later by the Hebrews, eventually by the Christians and even further by the Mohammedans" (Stone 196).

This stance, which was hostile to women, according to Stone, was taken by Christianity. She writes that "Woman, as sagacious advisor or wise counselor, human interpreter of the divine will of the Goddess, was no longer to be respected, but to be hated, feared or at best doubted or ignored." An example of this can be seen in St. Paul's epistles: "This demand for silence on the part of women, especially in the churches, is later reflected in the passages of Paul in the New Testament. According to the Judaic and Christian theology, woman's judgment had led to disaster for the whole human species." (Stone 221).

What Stone has in mind here are several passages written by St. Paul in which he clearly states that women should submit to their husbands. In *Ephesians*, he writes as follows:

> Wives, submit to your husbands as to
> the Lord.
> For the husband is the head of the
> wife as Christ is the head of the church,
> his body, of which he is the Savior.
> Now as the church submits to Christ,
> so also wives should submit to their
> husbands in everything.
> Husbands, love your wives, just as
> Christ loved the church and gave
> himself up for her. (Ephesians 5:22-25; New International Version)

These words cannot be disputed: St. Paul clearly says that men stand above women in the social hierarchy of that time. In I Timothy, he points out:

A woman should learn in quietness
and full submission.
I do not permit a woman to teach or to
have authority over a man; she must be
silent.
For Adam was formed first, then Eve.
And Adam was not the one deceived;
it was the woman who was deceived
and became a sinner. (I Timothy 2:11-14)

Here St. Paul is led by his lack of trust in the intelligence of women. They were perceived as having intellect lower than men. This was a prevailing prejudice at that time, and we can see it exposed in this passage. However, St. Paul never claimed that women are not human beings or that they must be enslaved. He says that men must respect women. A little bit further in I Timothy, we find the following passage:

Treat younger men as brothers,
older women as mothers, and younger
women as sisters, with absolute purity.
Give proper recognition to those
widows who are really in need. (I Timothy 5:1-3)

Therefore, only the intellectual abilities of women are rejected, but men are obliged to protect them, given that women's conduct is moral. In *Proverbs,* we read the following words regarding a wife of noble character:

> She is clothed with strength and dignity; she can laugh at the days to come.
> She speaks with wisdom, and faithful instruction is on her tongue.
> She watches over the affairs of her household and does not eat the bread of idleness. (Proverbs 31:25-27)

Not all women are of such noble character, but all women must still be respected if they are moral and pure. As this passage continues:

> Charm is deceptive, and beauty is fleeting; but a woman who fears the Lord is to be praised.
> Give her the reward she has earned, and let her works bring her praise at the city gate. (Proverbs 31:30-31)

Hence, it cannot be argued cogently that the Bible is full of passages against women in general; to do so would be a baseless reduction to absurdity. The more controversial passages express the spirit of that time. But as we noted, the Bible cannot solely be perceived literally[14], and one should study it carefully; otherwise, he/she will be led into a mistake.

The medieval Church, unfortunately, did not try to oppose these misunderstandings. As a result, the situation of women became hard, in a social and political sense. They were not slaves, but they were treated as unwise and unable to discuss proper theological issues. As Stone observes with sadness, “As the years went on and the position and status of women continued to lose ground, the Church held fast to its goals of creating and maintaining a male-dominated society” (Stone 224). Thus, she concludes, “Through the violent imposition and eventually forced acceptance of the male religions, women had finally been maneuvered into a role far removed from the ancient status they once held in the lands where the Queen of Heaven reigned” (Stone 228).

Merlin Stone’s conception is much more precise than Andrea Dworkin’s attempt for the philosophical reconstruction of past events. Dworkin directly accuses men that they intentionally enslaved women. On the other hand, Stone shows that men did not enslave women, but it was the “northern invaders” who transformed the society and eradicated the “female religion.” The goals of both feminists are different as well: whereas Dworkin dreams of a feminist revolution, Stone is eager to see the renewed interest in “female religion.”

---

[14] Holy Writ should be interpreted by the Bride of the Holy Spirit, the Holy Roman Catholic Church. Also, there is a fourfold sense to Scripture; literal, moral, allegorical and anagogical.

Based on their conception, the writer Dan Brown attempted to explain the eradication of "female religion" with the hypothesis that Jesus Christ had children and was married to Saint Mary Magdalene (Brown 329); because of this, the Catholic Church decided to repress all women and to suppress the idea of the Sacred Feminine, as the writer supposes. As Brown says in his *Da Vinci Code*, the Catholic Church's big secret is the "fact" that Christ had children and that He was not divine; Christ was simply a prophet. This position is expressed by two of the book's main characters: Leigh Teabing and Robert Langdon. According to them, the Holy Grail (or Sangreal) is a human being; initially, it was Saint Mary Magdalene; later, Holy Grail became a code word for Christ and Mary Magdalene's children.

In his conversation with Langdon and Sophie, Teabing says: "Not only was Jesus Christ married, but he was a father… Mary Magdalene was the Holy Vessel. She was the chalice that bore the royal bloodline of Jesus Christ" (Brown 336). In this sense, the Church has been hiding this significant secret from the believers. The result of revealing the secret would be the destruction and end of the Church.

The book's plot turns around this idea: there has always been a struggle between a small group of people believing in the Sacred Feminine with the Catholic Church, which has been trying to reject it and demonize it. In a conversation with Sophie, Langdon asserts: "Women, once celebrated as an essential half of spiritual enlightenment, had been banished from the temples of the world. There were no female Orthodox rabbis, Catholic priests, nor Islamic clerics." Following the ideas of Merlin Stone, he goes on: "The once hallowed act of Hieros Gamos—the natural sexual union between man and woman through which each became spiritually whole—had been recast as a shameful act" (Brown 173-4).

The small group of people fighting for the "truth" about Christ is called The Priory in the book. The Priory, according to his explanation, fights against the "distortion" of the ideas of Christ by the Catholic Church; this attempt for distortion dates back to Emperor Constantine (4th century). This secret organization "believes that Constantine and his male successors successfully converted the world from matriarchal paganism to patriarchal Christianity by waging a campaign of propaganda that demonized the sacred feminine, obliterating the goddess from modern religion" (Brown 172).

This conspiracy theory goes hand in hand with the hypothesis that Christ was actually not of divine origin and that all of the Apostles knew it. Christ was simply a prophet, and He never spoke of His divine origin. As Teabing says, "It was all about power… Christ as Messiah was critical to the functioning of Church and state… The early Church literally *stole* Jesus from his original followers, hijacking his human message" (Brown 316). In short, the history of Christianity and even the Bible itself can be explained only in terms of power and ambitions for gaining it.

There is nothing strange in this thesis- it is quite popular nowadays to accuse the Church of distorting the teaching of Christ. Modern atheists either reject the very existence of Christ or simply deny His divinity, thereby claiming that the idea of the Son of God was created later; that it was not present in the Bible initially. Some people from the Church, as we are informed, had to distort Christ's ideas in the name of power.

Emperor Constantine wanted to have substantial power residing in the divinity of Christ, so he commissioned the creation and popularization of the idea that Christ is God.

The Bible as we know it, Leigh Teabing says, is not the authentic Bible. He states that "Constantine commissioned and financed a new Bible, which omitted those gospels that spoke of Christ's *human* traits and embellished those gospels that made Him godlike" (Brown 317). In short, the Bible is not inspired by God but is man-made; it was created by people for other people. This leads to other questions: Are all stories described in the Bible fictitious? Langdon (that is, the author of the book- Dan Brown) says this is so. All stories there are not real; human-made is also the story of Original Sin, as Robert Langdon claims: "It was *man,* not God, who created the concept of 'original sin,' whereby Eve tasted of the apple and caused the downfall of the human race. Woman, once the sacred giver of life, was now the enemy" (Brown 321-2).

All this is a conspiracy of the Catholic Church against the ancient cults of the Goddess. Christians were against these cults because they were afraid of the influence of women. As Teabing and Langdon suggest, Saint Mary Magdalene had to be the successor of Christ instead of Saint Peter. So the Apostle Peter took things in his own hands and "eliminated" Saint Mary Magdalene from the Gospels. This is a pure conspiracy theory which is far from the facts.

Another example of this "conspiracy" is the symbol of the pentacle (pentagram). As a specialist in symbology, Langdon claims that it symbolizes nature; and nature was perceived as having two halves: "The ancients envisioned their world in two halves—masculine and feminine. Their gods and goddesses worked to keep a balance of power…When male and female were balanced, there was harmony in the world. When they were unbalanced, there was chaos" (Brown 60).[15] The pentacle was declared a satanic symbol in the past, Langdon claims, and because of this now it is still comprehended as such. Nevertheless, Langdon states that this does not seem right: the pentacle is simply part of the ancient worldview. Another part of the latter was the idea of the Sacred Feminine.

The plot of the da Vinci Code revolves around a mystery. Without a doubt, the book is an excellent thriller; however, Brown's hypothesis is pure fantasy, since it is not based on historical facts. Christianity was born during the time of Christ, and the Apostles followed Christ closely. Saint Peter never wanted to take power from Saint Mary Magdalene. It was impossible for one person to distort the whole teaching of Christ.

Moreover, the divinity of Christ and the fact that He was never married is not something "added" by the Church at a later time. These are historical facts. Nevertheless, some anonymous writings spoke about a possible marriage of Christ, but their authenticity cannot be proved. They contain fascinating ideas, but most of them were rejected by the majority of Christians. It is not true that the Council of Nicaea established the divinity of Christ; none of the Apostles had a doubt in the fact that Christ is the Son of God and that He resurrected from death.

At any rate, Dan Brown is right about one thing: that Christ showed respect toward women and femininity. This can be seen in several passages in the New Testament. It should be asserted that Christianity, at its core, is not against women. As we read in *Galatians*:

---

[15] The upward facing triangle represent women who have wider hips, and the downward facing triangle represents men who have wide shoulders.

> You are all sons of God through faith
> in Christ Jesus,
> for all of you who were baptized into
> Christ have clothed yourselves with
> Christ.
> There is neither Jew nor Greek, slave
> nor free, male nor female, for you are all
> one in Christ Jesus. (Galatians 3:26-28)

In God, we are all one; there are no real differences within Him. Our faith is what makes us one whole, one community. Before God, we are equal; men cannot stand above women simply because all human beings are finite and sinful. All of us bear the burden of Original Sin. Men and women suffer equally. With this passage, it becomes clear that St. Paul never showed disrespect for women and femininity. Let us check this hypothesis more in detail in the following subchapter.

4.2 Christianity and women. The Blessed Virgin Mary as the archetype of femininity

Summary:

The Christian understanding of womanhood and femininity is associated with the Blessed Virgin Mary. She covers all the positive aspects of femininity. To some extent, she can be opposed to Eve, who was a sinner. Therefore, Christianity does not accuse women of committing the Original Sin. It understands them in the light of the life and deeds of the Blessed Virgin Mary.

The views presented by Merlin Stone are based on historical pieces of evidence. There is nothing strange in the fact that ancient cults of the Goddess existed in the distant past. However, we showed that Dan Brown's hypothesis is pure mystification; that there are not any proofs of his assumption that the Catholic Church intentionally "has hidden" the truth about Christ. There are no passages in the New Testament, indicating that Christ had a family and a wife. Furthermore, the fact that women were initially equal to men in the apostolic mission is easy to explain: all believers were welcome because Christianity was a new religion and needed to spread quickly. Once it was declared the official religion of the Roman Empire, the number of missionaries decreased. Correspondingly, women were denied further participation in this mission. This was due probably to their lack of education as well as the attitude of the society at that time. As we already said, this attitude was wrong, but it is a fact, and we cannot change this fact now. The question is whether Christianity itself is anti-women, against women.

Lynne Marie Kohm and her fellow researchers in their article on Christianity and feminism admit that the Church used to have a negative attitude toward women's rights. Moreover, they do not write about the priesthood, which is entirely reserved for men. The good news is that theological education became open to women, although as late as in the 20th century. A real achievement "is the increased opportunity for women's ordination and ministry leadership. Although women's ordination may seem like a relatively new phenomenon, the history of ordination goes back to the first century church" (Kohm et al.

7). As the authors state, in spite of the fact that the Catholic Church does not allow women to be ordained, "several denominations have ordained women, including the Salvation Army, Pentecostal Holiness Church, Church of the Nazarene, and Open Bible Standard Churches." To them, we can add other non-Catholic Churches which "initiated rule changes that permitted women's ordination including the Wesleyan Methodist Church, African Methodist Episcopal Zion Church, Baptist General Conference, Assemblies of God, Presbyterian Church of the U.S.A., Episcopal Church" (Kohm et al. 9). Thus, the general attitude toward women is more favourable than in the past. However, the authors claim that there is a lot to do in this direction, and women should be allowed to deal more with theological and church issues. This is an average ambition that stems from the fact that women today have all the rights men have.

All this does not mean that Christianity has achieved real gender equality. The authors point to the mentality of some priests and believers who are convinced that women must submit to their husbands. They rely on the passages in the epistles of St. Paul, which we quoted earlier. In the past, Kohm and her fellows write, "Some viewed being created in the image of God (i.e., Lat., imago Dei), a theological theme dominating Western thought, as meaning that women lack the image of God and only coalesce with God's image if they are under male headship" (Kohm et al. 5). This attitude was challenged by the theologian Karl Barth, who "asserted that 'the imago Dei relates to God creating humankind as male and female in cohumanity in order to respond to God's Word.' Therefore, men and women are formed in the image of God by having a synergistic relationship with one another" (Kohm et al. 5).

The Catholic Church says something similar today. Women are equal to men in all respects. This is what has changed, the authors observe.

Nevertheless, is something like Christian feminism possible today? Can Christians be feminists? Of course, they can. This would be the type of feminism endorsed by Mary Wollstonecraft. This is pure feminism, not affiliated with atheism or materialism. In its initial form, feminism is compatible with Christianity, the authors say. However, contemporary feminism stands against Christianity. There is an evident hostility between both camps. As Kohm and her research team remark, the real debate is not there; both sides do not want to listen to each other. The researchers say that "What is glaringly absent from the dialogue on gender in the church is an authentic sense of repentance and forgiveness needed on both sides of the debate" (Kohm et al. 17). A real dialogue is needed, not a war.

The Church has the opportunity to get some facts about both genders straight: "In an era of gender confusion, devaluation, and political correctness, the church has the opportunity to enact a restorative and biblical understanding of true gender identity" (Kohm et al. 17). We can add that this conception should not be based on biology, as wrongly some believers do nowadays. It happens very often that the claims of transgenderism (as a doctrine) are repudiated by referring to the evolution theory and biology. This is a misinterpretation of the Christian notion of nature. For Christianity, nature is what we have from the very beginning, from the act of Creation onwards. Nature is not the material world or physical nature. Any explanation of the fact that only two genders exist must begin with God and with the idea of man as an image of God.

Without any doubt, the Christian worldview stands above contemporary feminism. It offers a stable explanation of all social and political processes which we witness. Christianity offers a set of values in a world full of existential vacuums and which lacks moral ideals. Nevertheless, where is the woman in this world of Christian values? Is she really discriminated against?

Women are understood as having a unique role in our society. They are symbols of tenderness, love, and empathy. They are associated with altruism. In this sense, they must be respected, not ridiculed. Even though not all women become mothers (for one reason or another), they can be mothers in another sense- that they protect or take care of someone else (brothers, parents, close relatives, orphans, etc.). Christianity thus sees women as the beginning of human life on earth. Women symbolize compassion and love.

Unlike feminism, Christianity does not say that man is absolutely free. We are endowed with free will, but our freedom is restricted by morality. Humans cannot live without moral values. Even radical feminism has its own ideals (although they are weird and even dangerous). Furthermore, we live in a community; feminism emphasizes the individual, which is wrong. The Christian community is much stronger and more stable than the radical feminist person. The fact that feminism has so many forms indicates that feminists cannot build their own community. They do not have the basis for it- the moral basis.

The ideal of womanhood and femininity in Christianity is associated with the Blessed Virgin Mary, the Mother of God. In contrast with the ideal of feminism- masculine, strong women, with plenty of ambitions and plans for a professional career- we see here, compassion, altruism, love, and forgiveness. *The Blessed Virgin Mary is what feminism cannot stand and bear because she is "too feminine" for them.* As Kohm and her team observe, she "as a woman of faith and agent of God's salvation, stands in the unique role of being the mother of the Son of God, forever contributing to the dignity of motherhood, and serving as a biblical exemplar for gender equality." They assert that "Because of Mary, God did not stand at a distance from humankind but rather extended his existence to us in the person of Jesus Christ" (Kohm et al. 10).

In what sense is the Blessed Virgin Mary a model for all women and for femininity? In order to answer this question, we have to emphasize two important points: first, Holy Mary is the opposite of Eve; and second, she is the opposite of the ancient Goddess Mother. The first point will be analyzed further in this opus. Now we will take the second one.

The ancient Goddess was seen as the patron of fertility and agriculture. She was associated with sexuality and children. As we noted, some female deities were also warriors, but this was a rare case. The so-called "sacred prostitution" was practiced in the name of the Goddess. This was a ritual which was understood as uniting heaven and earth, male and female, in the name of fertility and life. It is shocking that people practiced it in the name of religion, but this is a historical fact.

The "female religion" was pagan in many aspects. It consisted of beliefs in many gods, in the existence of demons and evil spirits, in the idea that all material things have souls (animism). But most importantly, it posited the existence of a direct relationship between the cult practices and some natural phenomena. For example, these rituals could lead to rain if needed, as it was believed.

Christianity opposed this understanding with the idea that God stands above and beyond gender; God is neither He nor She. However, we speak of Him in a metaphorical way, and because our language demands so. There are no practices which can make Him send rain to the earth; God is a personal entity, but He is also abstract since He cannot be described by our language. God is thus personal and impersonal at once; He can be and cannot be defined.

The Blessed Virgin Mary is comprehended as the Mother of God, but not in the sense that she created the world or existed before the world. Jesus Christ is the Son of God, Who had to descend to earth to redeem humanity. The Blessed Virgin is His Mother; she gave birth to the Second Person of the Most Holy Trinity. This is important if we want to understand what is her role in and for Christianity. One of the reasons for attacking the title Mother of God was precisely this: that God cannot be born, God was never born. Nevertheless, this objection is rooted in a misunderstanding of the role of the Blessed Virgin Mary.

The Blessed Virgin Mary is not a separate deity. She is not a remnant of the ancient cult of the Goddess. No one can prove that there is a connection between her and the ancient Goddess (in Egypt, Sumer, Babylon, etc.). Because she is a virgin, she stands as the opposite of the Goddess, in whose name plenty of sexual acts were performed. Thus, on the one side, we encounter virginity and purity (The Ever-Virgin Mother of God); on the other side, decay and fornication (Goddess).

The belief in the evil spirits characterized pagan religions. Some rituals were performed to make them more benevolent toward people. In such a way, good and evil were seen as interconnected and mutually dependent. Christianity, on the contrary, draws a bold line between good and evil. God is love; and Holy Mary, the Mother of God, is charity and compassion. She is like the Mother (in a symbolic sense) of the whole humankind, of all people that existed, exist, and will exist. Because of all this, the prayers of Christians are also directed through Her and the Saints, to God.

Another significant opposition can be seen between the Blessed Virgin and Eve from Eden. Friar Andre Marie observes in his article about the Blessed Virgin that Christian theology has always seen her as the opposition of Eve. Many theologians have made an analogy between Adam and Christ, and Eve and the Blessed Virgin Mary. As Friar Marie puts it, "Jesus Christ is the New Adam. Now, the old Adam had a helpmate like unto himself who was his partner in crime. It's a parallelism that begs to be completed. Common sense tells us we don't have to look far to complete it." He goes on by adding that "the Gospels show us that Jesus had a partner in redemption, and that partner was Mary" (Marie par. 2).

All this should not be taken literally. We noted earlier that any literal reading of the Bible could lead to misunderstandings. An analogy between Adam and Jesus Christ should not be perceived as meaning that Christ was only a human being (since Adam was solely a human being). Nevertheless, one cannot help thinking that Adam can be opposed to Christ: Adam is the sinner, and Christ is the Redeemer. Something similar could be said about Eve and the Mother of God. Eve is not an absolute opposition to the Blessed Virgin Mary, but she is still culpable because of the temptation to which she succumbed.

Friar Andre Marie is led in his reflections by the words of St. Paul in a few of his epistles. Marie observes that "Saint Paul provides us with the first part of our argument. It is this inspired title of Jesus Christ: The Last Adam. In two passages, the Blessed Apostle teaches us that Adam was a type 1 of Our Lord as the head of a new race." As he goes on, "As Adam was the head of fallen humanity, Christ Our Lord is head of a regenerated, sanctified humanity" (Marie par. 3). Then he quotes two passages: one from *Romans* and one from 1 *Corinthians*. In *Romans*, we read the following:

> For if, by the trespass of the one man,
> death reigned through that one man,
> how much more will those who receive
> God's abundant provision of grace and
> of the gift of righteousness reign in life
> through the one man, Jesus Christ. (Romans 5:17)

Here we see a direct opposition between Adam and Christ, of the first man to the Son of God. St. Paul explains that God's Grace is really great because He sent His Son to sacrifice Him for us.

Another contrast is seen in 1 *Corinthians*:

> So it is written: 'The first man Adam
> became a living being'; the last Adam,
> a lifegiving spirit.
> The spiritual did not come first, but the
> natural, and after that the spiritual.
> The first man was of the dust of the

> earth, the second man from heaven. (1 Corinthians 15:45-47)

All this means that we are not entirely material beings but that there is something spiritual in us. We are in touch with God, with the divine. We are not wholly finite beings; there is a spiritual substance which approximates us to God. As St. Paul goes on:

> And just as we have borne the
> likeness of the earthly man, so shall we
> bear the likeness of the man from
> heaven. (1 Corinthians 15:49)

Therefore, there is some logic in contrasting Adam to Christ. In the same sense, the Blessed Virgin Mary is to be contrasted to Eve. Hence, Eve is not the symbol of womanhood, or at least, she is not the only symbol.

As Friar Andre Marie remarks, the conception of the Blessed Virgin Mary as the opposite of Eve (the sinner) has been developed over time by Christian theologians. He points out that Saint Justin Martyr was the first theologian who turned to this analogy: "It is likely that this great philosopher-martyr was referring to an older tradition when he made the following reference, contrasting Mary's Annunciation with Eve's encounter with the serpent" (Marie par. 9). Friar Marie states that the role of the Blessed Virgin Mary has always been considered very important. She is the mediator between God and man. As Friar Marie remarks, plenty of patristic theologians "assign to the Virgin an active role in man's salvation. She was no mere passive recipient of grace…Here is Saint

Irenaeus of Lyons, who tells us that Mary is the 'cause of salvation,' whereas Eve had been the 'cause of death'" (Marie par. 12).

Someone may say that such an analogy is not right. Eve has been perceived as the perpetrator of Original Sin, but she was not alone in this. Adam was her collaborator in sinning. Adam and Eve together symbolize human sinfulness. As Friar Marie explains, "Here we need to repeat what many are probably unaware of, namely, that it was Adam's sin, not Eve's, which is the original sin" (Marie par. 14).

There is some truth in the rejection of such an analogy. The Blessed Virgin Mary, the Mother of God, was not born to redeem Original Sin. Christ is the Redeemer Who helped us find the way to God and our salvation. Christ never spoke of Eve as connected to His Mother.

What is essential for us in this possible analogy is the womanhood expressed by the Mother of God. She is not a deity; she is not divine herself. During her earthly existence, the Blessed Virgin Mary was a woman, a human being. Unlike Christ, she did not have two natures- one human and one divine.

Mary is the symbol of womanhood in the sense that she covers all positive aspects of being a woman in this world. She is a Virgin; She is the Mother of God; She suffered because of Him and His death; She was one of the first persons to know about His Resurrection. She is compassionate and kind; because of all this, Christians believe that She is the mediator between man and God, and She is the distributor of His Graces.

In some sense, Eve is also the mother of humankind. Thus, the analogy can be carried out between her and Holy Mary. A significant scene to be noted is the suffering of the Blessed Virgin Mary near the cross of Christ, Her Son. Friar Andre Marie writes that

"Perhaps the most beautifully developed aspect of the Eve-Mary parallel is that of Our Lady as the Sorrowful Mother. Beginning in the middle ages, learned men 'connected the dots' between Eden and Calvary to show the many correspondences" (Marie par. 35). Theologians realized that Mary's place in Christ's mission is not insignificant: "If Mary was a 'helpmate' to Jesus in the Redemption of man, and if Jesus redeemed us on the Cross, then Mary's standing at the foot of the Cross must be more than just coincidence" (Marie par. 35).

As a matter of fact, it is not important whether this analogy is accurate; it is not crucial whether God had any plan to compensate the wrong deeds of Eve with the deeds of the Blessed Virgin Mary, the Mother of God. Our goal here is not to study this analogy in detail. The majority of theologians agree that Eve and the Blessed Virgin Mary should be seen as opposing each other. It is vital for us to realize that the Blessed Virgin Mary is associated with femininity. *The Blessed Virgin Mary covers all positive aspects of femininity and womanhood, and we should not understand her role as merely opposing Eve. She was not born because of Eve's sin; the Blessed Virgin Mary had a completely different mission: to be the Mother of the Son of God.*

Thus, the Christian conception of femininity and women is based on the idea that *the Blessed Virgin Mary has in Her all positive features and traits related to womanhood. All women should follow Her example in being compassionate altruistic, caring, loving. They should take care of their children and love their husbands*; at the same time, they should not have any egoistic desires and ambitions. Women are idealized in Christianity: the woman is seen as a moral ideal, not as a subhuman, as some atheists want to persuade us.

Nonetheless, someone may object as follows: this attitude toward women is not the same as perceiving them as equal. If we idealize women and say that all they should be altruistic and loving and caring, then what about men? Should men be allowed to be egoists and do whatever they want?

Christianity does not perceive women as separate beings from men. We are one in the sense that we were created by God. Adam and Eve were one; they existed in harmony. There are many examples of harmonious couples in the Bible. Both women and men are human beings; this is the essential idea of Christianity. Now, *contemporary feminism tries to show that women are entirely different in any possible respect. It makes men and women go against each other*; it provokes unwise discussions regarding both genders' roles. The Christian standpoint says that first we are human, and then we are men and women. Feminism says that we are either men or women in an absolute sense, and there cannot be connections between us.

We already noted that Christianity could have some fruitful communication with feminism, provided that the latter becomes less radical and admits its mistakes. Feminists could be Christians, but they should respect our faith in God. There is nothing wrong in saying that one is a feminist unless this one has said something terrible about Christianity. *A possible theory of Christian feminism should be founded upon the conception of Holy Mary. Women should not search for liberation from "male domination" but from sin and wrongdoing*. Both men and women are responsible for this liberation. The assumption that men dominate our society in a wrong way distracts us from our main task: to get rid of sin and evil.

There is another point to be analyzed as regards the Christian worldview of women and womanhood. Why were we created men and women? Why isn't there only one gender? Why not more than two? One ancient philosopher discusses this question.

4.3 The myth of the androgynous humans

Summary:

This short subchapter deals with the myth of Aristophanes told in the dialogue *Symposium* by Plato. It shows that the theory of androgynous humans is not compatible with Christianity.

Perhaps the reader has read about the idea that once humans were one whole, called androgynous men, and later this whole was split into two parts- men and women. This idea comes from Plato's philosophy, more particularly from his *Symposium.* This is one of the most remarkable dialogues of Plato. The problem of love is discussed comprehensively there.

Plato introduces this idea as a *myth.* We should comprehend it as an *allegory* with which Plato wants to tell us something. Here we will try to interpret his view without denying the existence of alternative explanations.

The "androgynous man hypothesis", as we could call it, is not compatible with Christianity for many reasons. But before analyzing them, let us see what is written in this dialogue of Plato.

The myth is told by Aristophanes, a famous writer, whose speech, however, is produced by Plato himself.[16] In his speech, Aristophanes says that in the distant past, there were three genders, not two: "There was man and woman, and the union of the two, having a name corresponding to this double nature, which had once a real existence, but is now lost, and the word 'androgynous' is only preserved as a term of reproach" (Plato 178-9). All of these human beings were strong and had grand ambitions, due to which they stood against the gods: "Terrible was their might and strength, and the thoughts of their hearts were great, and they made an attack upon the gods" (Plato 179). The gods decided not to annihilate them but to teach them a lesson. Zeus said: "Men shall continue to exist, but I will cut them in two and then they will be diminished in strength and increased in numbers; this will have the advantage of making them more profitable to us. They shall walk upright on two legs" (Plato 179). Then men were divided into two halves; women into two halves; and the androgynous persons into two halves. In this way, their strength decreased. However, the result of all this was that these beings were eager to meet their other half. As Aristophanes goes on, "each desiring his other half, came together, and throwing their arms about one another, entwined in mutual embraces, longing to grow into one; they were on the point of dying from hunger and self-neglect, because they did not like to do anything apart" (Plato 180). This is his explanation of romantic love: we are in a constant search of our "other half." As the narrative continues, "Each of us when separated, having one side only, like a flat fish, is but the indenture of a man, and he is always looking for his other half" (Plato 180).

[16] In his dialogues, Plato often uses real characters, but he inserts his own words in their mouth. The best example of this is Socrates.

The conclusion of all this is that human beings were one harmonic whole; they were not aware of how nice this was. Humans needed to become separated from each other to understand the truth. The truth is that love is the supreme power in this world. As Plato says through the mouth of Aristophanes, "human nature was originally one and we were a whole, and the desire and pursuit of the whole is called love" (Plato 182). Love is the strongest god existing in this world; love is stronger than all Olympic gods. This initial state should be our dream; we have to turn back to our roots, and love can help us do it: "I believe that if our loves were perfectly accomplished, and each one returning to his primeval nature had his original true love, then our race would be happy" (Plato 182).

This romantic explanation, however, stands close to paganism and the pagan worldview. It actually rejects the role of the Divine and says that there is no God, and only men can be gods. The myth of the androgynous men was borrowed (maybe unintentionally) by Shulamith Firestone and Andrea Dworkin. In their attempt to depict the society of the future, they turned to Plato's myth about the existence of androgynous human beings. Therefore, they did not create this hypothesis.

From the Christian standpoint, the idea of the androgynous people must be firmly rejected. What are the reasons for such rejection? Why should we not accept the idea that men and women are like two halves of one whole? What is wrong in that?

Let us turn for a while to the Chinese conception of Ying and Yang. The male and female coexist in harmony, but they do it through struggle. Taoism (from which this conception stems) is based on the idea that harmony is a struggle and mutual rejection. Thus, the male is defined through the female; and vice versa. Men and women are not independent beings; they are mutually dependent.

All this seems nice, but there is one difficulty here. It takes men and women first as representatives of their particular sex, not as human beings. The approach to them is not universal but segregated. Why were men and women created as men and women? The answer of Plato is that men and women were one whole, and they were split later into halves; the Chinese would say that men and women are still one whole, but this unity is invisible to us.

The unity of men and women is rooted in the fact that they are created by God, by the only existing Divine Being. It is not a matter of romantic love. Plato's conception (rather a myth) is romantic and poetic, but it is not realistic. Love is a nice feeling, but its interpretation is wrong. Especially in the *Symposium*, love is seen as *eros* rather than as *agape* or *agathon*. *Agathon* is the good, which ancient Greeks saw as identical with the beautiful and the true. *Agape* is the selfless love (charity), which is praised in Christianity as one of the supreme values. Thus, *Plato's mistake is that he eroticized the conception of love; and with this, he puts emphasis on the sexual relations between men and women.* Contemporary feminism derives its sexualized conception precisely from pagan practices and ideas. This can be seen when one traces the connection between Shulamith's androgynous society and the myth of Aristophanes.

An androgynous human being is impossible to imagine. Perhaps technologies can create something similar to it, but it would be rather an artificial being. We cannot accept the idea that in the distant past, men and women were one whole, and somehow the genders appeared (in spite of the fact that even Plato says that men and women existed then).

Another important ramification of the myth of Aristophanes is the apology of homosexuality. This myth is often used to explain that homosexual relations are also romantic relations and that this is “true love.” This is, again, an attempt to sexualize the problem of gender. Men and women are much more than mere biological beings; we are not merely natural instincts; we have a spiritual substance which must be taken into account by any anthropological theory.

At any rate, humankind does not need androgynous human beings. Men and women perform their roles quite well. All we need to do is simply to be humans and then to be men and women. Whether we are men or women, we should feel compassion and love all other humans on earth. Compassion and charity are not “women’s things”, but they concern us all.

The positive conclusion of the myth of Aristophanes is that we can do everything when we are united; that we are strong only together. Moreover, this should be said about the whole Christian community. By extending it further, we will include more and more persons, and we will become stronger than before. Nevertheless, all the time we should keep our humbleness and meekness; instead of reaching out for Olympus (trying to become gods), we have to realize that we are simply finite beings; we are mortal and deprived of supernatural powers. The story of the Tower of Babel demonstrates that people should not be too proud; they need to understand what is their role in the world and why they were created. People should not stand against God; they should not fight with each other.

Plato’s philosophy is almost entirely pagan. It incorporates many ideas typical of ancient Greek religion. In spite of the fact that medieval theologians had respect for him,

Plato still remains a pagan philosopher. Consequently, his myth of the androgynous humans should be seen as part of the pagan worldview, and maybe as related to the cult of the Goddess. Christians need to stay away from such ideas; although it is very romantic to believe in the theory of the "two halves," it does not have anything to do with Christianity.

4.4 Conclusion

Christianity has been attacked on many fronts. It has been accused of discrimination against women and depriving women of their rights. Contemporary feminists are usually militant atheists. As we saw in this book, some of them endorse Islam and claim that Islam offers pro-women practices. There are many absurdities in their writings, including the ideas of marriage with children and the destruction of the family in general.

The Christian standpoint is clear: it offers an understanding of the relations between men and women by showing their connection with the family. Romantic relations naturally are incorporated in marriage and children. To be a man is to love and take care of other humans; to be a woman is the same. Men should not love less simply because they are men.

What feminists do not like in Christianity is the idea that there is a Divine power above them. They want to have their life only for them; they do not care about other humans, about the meaning of life or the origin of this world. They do not care about life after death. At the same time, they offer us a utopia- the conception of a future society without gender differences, without family and even without states (as political entities).

Modern feminism does not provide us with an alternative model to Christianity. They do not offer real, long-lasting moral values. Feminists need to be meeker, to admit their mistakes and to try to reform their movement, which began two centuries ago, but now is very far from its initial ambitions and premises.

Chapter V: Conclusion

This short overview of feminist philosophy cannot claim to comprise all possible aspects of feminism. We have omitted many more names in the field of feminism. By emphasizing the teaching of Shulamith Firestone and Andrea Dworkin, we intended to show how feminism looks like generally. However, feminism, as we already explained in the beginning, cannot be seen as a homogenous philosophy. There are many internal divisions in it. As we saw, some feminists have sympathies for Islam; others do not have such. Some feminists are "sex-negative," others are "sex-positive." Some feminists argue in favor of lesbianism, and others think that heterosexual relations are OK. Nevertheless, generally, feminism nowadays revolves around the view that men still are dominating society, and they must be replaced by women. Women should take (almost) all political power in the world and should deal more with business and all other spheres of human activity.

We already noted that feminism is not wrong if taken in itself. The feminism of Wollstonecraft is remarkable, but it is not real feminism. Here we will not discuss the term "feminism" as deep as to say whether Wollstonecraft was a "feminist." We simply accept that she was such. *Feminism, however, has gone too far: it has turned into political philosophy and even a political movement*. This does not seem right; this is unacceptable if we take into account what first feminists demanded. Yes, they wanted more political rights for women; but these rights are granted to them now. *Let us tell the truth here: feminism has become an integral part of contemporary (socialist) liberalism*. Feminists and liberals agree that everyone can do whatever one wants; there is no morality; all social norms are conventional, i.e., they can be changed according to our individual needs and wishes.

Nevertheless, the most common point of these ideologies is the attack on religion: religion, they say, should be abandoned in the distant past; we do not need Christianity anymore. Christian values are against women, against the interest of women. Therefore, Christianity has to be eradicated or at least marginalized (to decrease its significance in our society).

This is perhaps the most disappointing view which we have seen in feminism. Christianity is not antifeminine. It never said that women have to be disrespected. Even if we take the words of St. Paul saying that women should remain silent literally, this still does not mean that women should not be loved. Christianity today takes care of women much more than any political or social organization or institution. All social activities of the Catholic Church (as well as Protestant churches) worldwide are directed to the well-being of women, and all human beings in general. The Church fights against poverty, discrimination, social injustice. The Church offers spiritual reassurance; it makes the faithful more confident.

All problems which are faced by women today can be solved by turning to Christianity and its values. The Christian society is based on values; there is no moral vacuum in it. The place of all us is in the Church; then comes the family, and then comes the society. By destroying one of them, we will destroy the other two elements. That is, our civilization will be under attack. Only by adhering firmly to the Christian values, which have helped us survive for so long, can we guarantee that human civilization will survive intact.

The last thing to be said here is that women themselves do not have trust in feminism. The surveys that we referred to earlier show that feminism is not seen well by most women in the United States (and we can say, in the whole world). Furthermore, the reason for this is not the influence of the Catholic Church. On the contrary: the problem is that *feminism has become too radical to be respected. The arguments of feminism stand far from sound logic*; there is too much anger and emotions in the words of feminists. Only by rejecting the radical ideas of Dworkin and Firestone can feminism become a widespread movement.

Feminism has accomplished its task, and it is not needed anymore. Women are granted the same rights granted to men. Here we speak only about women in the United States and Europe. Feminism can fight for women's rights in Africa or Muslim countries in Asia, but this is another topic. It is time to say goodbye to feminism and to leave its screaming proponents aside.

Works cited

Aossey, Gabby. Muslims Are the True Feminists. *Huffpost*, 11 May 2017. <www.huffpost.com/entry/muslims-are-the-true-feminists_b_9877692?>

The Bible. New International Version.

Bindel, Julie. Marriage Should be Abolished. The Civil Partnership Debate Proves That. *The Guardian*, 29 June 2018. (referred to as Marriage) <https://www.theguardian.com/commentisfree/2018/jun/29/marriage-abolished-civil-partnerships-inequality>

Bindel, Julie. Why Are So Many Left-Wing Progressives Silent About Islam's Totalitarian Tendencies? *UnHerd*, 3 April 2018. (referred to as UnHerd) <unherd.com/2018/04/many-left-wing-progressives-protest-pope-silent-islams-totalitarian-tendencies-victims-cowardice-overwhelmingly-women>

Bindel, Julie. Muslim Women Deserve Better Than Sharia Law. *Standpoint*, 23 Sep 2014. (referred to as Standpoint) <standpointmag.co.uk/features-october-14-muslim-women-deserve-better-than-sharia-law-julie-bindel-feminism>

Brown, Dan. *Da Vinci Code*. Corgi Books, 2003.

Cameron, Jessica Joy. *Reconsidering Radical Feminism. Affect and the Politics of Heterosexuality*. Vancouver and Toronto, UBC Press, 2018.

Campbell, Karlyn Kohrs. "Femininity and Feminism: To be or Not to be a Woman". *Communication Quarterly*, 31(2), 1983, pp. 101-108.

Catechism of the Catholic Church. <https://www.vatican.va/archive/ENG0015/_INDEX.HTM>

Clements, Barbara Evans. "Continuities Amid Change: Gender Ideas and Arrangements in Twentieth-Century Russia and Eastern Europe." Meade, Theresa A.; Merry Wiesner-Hanks (ed.) *A Companion to Gender History*, pp. 555-567. Blackwell, 2004.

Dworkin, Andrea. *Woman Hating*. Plume, 1974.

Firestone, Shulamith. *The Dialectic of Sex. The Case for Feminist Revolution*. A Bantam Book, 1970.

Fuller, Margaret. *Woman in the Nineteenth Century*. Boston and Cleveland, 1855.

Gray, Alex. These are the Countries Where Child Marriages are Legal. *World Economic Forum*, 26 September 2016 <https://www.weforum.org/agenda/2016/09/these-are-the-countries-where-child-marriage-is-legal/>

Kohm, Lynne Marie; Chandler, Diane; Gomez, Doris. "Christianity, Feminism, and the Paradox of Female Happiness." *17 Trinity L. Review* 191, 2011. <https://dx.doi.org/10.2139/ssrn.2001387>

Madison G., Aasa U., Wallert J. and Woodley M.A. (2014) "Feminist Activist Women are Masculinized in Terms of Digit-ratio and Social Dominance: A Possible Explanation for the Feminist Paradox." *Frontiers of Psychology* 5, 2014, article 1011. <doi:10.3389/fpsyg.2014.01011>

Brother Marie, Andre. "The Second Eve." *Catholicism*, 12 September 2005. <https://catholicism.org/second-eve.html>

Offen, Karen. "Defining Feminism: A Comparative Historical Approach." *Signs*, Vol. 14, No. 1. (Autumn, 1988), pp. 119-157.

Plato. "Symposium." *Five Great Dialogues*, pp. 155- 214. Translated by B. Jowett. D. Van Nostrand Company, Toronto, New York, London, 1942.

Stone, Merlin. *When God Was a Woman*. HBJ, San Diego, New York, London, 1976.

Winslow, Barbara. "Feminist Movements: Gender and Sexual Equality."

Meade, Theresa A.; Merry Wiesner-Hanks (ed.) *A Companion to Gender History*, pp. 186-205, Blackwell, 2004.

Wollstonecraft, Mary. *A Vindication of the Rights of Woman*. New York, A. J. Matsell, 1833.

www.ingramcontent.com/pod-product-compliance
Lightning Source LLC
LaVergne TN
LVHW082246150826
845677LV00009B/1543

* 9 7 9 8 8 6 9 1 8 1 1 2 1 *